111 Comforting GLUTEN-FREE, GRAIN-FREE, and DAIRY-FREE RECIPES for THE FOODIE in YOU

PALEO EATS

KELLY BEJELLY

Victory Belt Publishing Inc.
Las Vegas

First published in 2014 by Victory Belt Publishing Inc.

ISBN-13: 978-1-628600-43-8

Interior design by Yordan Terziev and Boryana Yordanova
Cover portrait and photos on pages 8 and 10 by Crystal Genes Photography

Printed in the U.S.A.
RRD 0114

To my son, The Little

You turned my world right-side up, drew flowers all over the walls with purple crayons, and then left muddy handprints on my heart. Thank you for choosing me to be part of your journey.

Contents

Foreword
by Liz Wolfe, NTP
bestselling author of *Eat the Yolks*

 For my first few years as a Paleo eater, I didn't think I had an ounce of "foodie" in me. I was lucky if I could figure out how to grill a hamburger. Organic ketchup covers all manner of food-related sins, right?

It was even worse prior to Paleo. Long before I became brave enough to fire up the grill, I relied heavily on prepackaged junk for the majority of my meals—including junk disguised as "health food" that made me *believe* I was doing something good for myself. I'd eat a packet of berries-and-cream-flavored instant oatmeal for breakfast, a "healthy whole-grain" meal-replacement bar for lunch, and a weight-loss-branded microwave meal for dinner, followed, of course, by a pint of soy ice cream, a few of my roommates' low-calorie snack packs, and several hours of wallowing in my own diet failures. My indulgences were low-carb packaged "treats" that tasted of cardboard and nightmares, and the concept of comfort food struck fear into my heart.

When I started Paleo, I saw incredible improvements in my skin, hair, body composition, and self-image from ditching all that prepackaged junk, but I *still* viewed food in a context of punishment and slip-ups. Enjoying rich, robust food, even the Paleo-friendly kind, still felt . . . well, *wrong,* and "comfort food" remained a fearsome, dirty term.

It was years before I truly understood that good, rich, flavorful food isn't to be feared, that we can nourish ourselves while enjoying the food that fuels us, and that feeding the senses with well-made, comforting food doesn't have to mean weeks of guilt and atonement. I have people like Kelly Bejelly to thank for that realization. The tagline of her website is "Paleo cooking from the heart," and she lives up to that motto in *Paleo Eats.*

My first encounter with Kelly's blog, *A Girl Worth Saving,* came at the perfect time. I had begun to suspect that I could actually enjoy robust, flavorful, Paleo-friendly food without feeling guilty, *and* that I could make it myself without having to douse it in ketchup, but I was in dire need of a community of like-minded people. Kelly wasted no time bringing me into the fold of a group of healthy, creative foodies who enjoyed amazing, comforting, delicious food in good health. Inspiring people, for sure!

I found a kindred spirit in Kelly. She loves food, and she loves to share that love with others, but she also has very little patience for overly complicated, tricky recipes where the work outweighs the reward. Her simple, fresh, easy recipes do what food *should* do: keep us healthy, nourish our bodies, activate *all* our senses, and thereby feed our souls.

Kelly once told me, "There are few things that stimulate all five senses like food does—no wonder it's a love affair for so many people." The recipes in this book, from Coconut Cinnamon Cereal and Banana Pancakes to Apple Fritters, Southern Fried Chicken, Green Bean Casserole, and Kitchen Sink Cookies, are simply perfection, feeding not just the body but all the senses and the soul. Kelly creates such awesome flavor profiles that even kids, as picky as they can sometimes be, love her recipes!

The challenge—one that Kelly tackles head-on in this book—is helping people realize that this love affair with food isn't wrong, dangerously indulgent, or too much work; in fact, it's as easy and as healthy as it is delicious. What's more, a "foodie" doesn't have to be a person who loves complex recipes, fancy ingredients, and complicated cooking techniques. A foodie is a person *just like me (and just like you!)* who loves, respects, and enjoys good food.

Kelly shows us these truths deliciously and simply on every page of *Paleo Eats.* You'll love this book!

My Paleo Story

Can you imagine spending the rest of your life without experiencing the simple joy of a cookie? I can't. I may have saved myself from a host of mental and physical complaints when I adopted a Paleo diet, but that didn't mean I was willing to turn my back on my memories of cooking up something sweet in the kitchen with my mom. I will never forget that cake is a must-have for any birthday or that pizza can make family night just a tad more special.

Happy food memories are as much a part of me as my eye color, but in 2009, when my health was failing me and I heard the word *prediabetic*, I was desperate enough to try the Paleo diet. At the time, I was severely obese and suffering from daily panic attacks, and when I was told I was prediabetic, I was terrified that I would be sentenced to spend the rest of my days in the place I hated most: the doctor's office. Ever since I was a little girl, I have been afraid of going to the doctor. Doctors meant needles and fourteen-letter medications with side effects worse than the problem I was trying to cure. When I realized that I was going to have to take insulin and see a doctor every three months, I lost it and completely broke down.

The good thing about hitting rock bottom is that it drove home that I needed to make a change, and I was motivated to figure out how to heal myself through diet. When I stopped eating grains and legumes, I lost sixty-five pounds effortlessly, ended my daily battle with anxiety and night terrors, and reduced my dependency on Western medicine.

My story starts out the same as that of most people who find themselves on the Paleo diet. In college, I went from being a meat-loving carnivore—as in, I ate some type of meat at every single meal—to being a vegetarian. It was one of the worst mistakes of my life, and if I could go back in time and slap my younger self, I would. Admittedly, I wasn't a *good* vegetarian: Most of my meals were centered on carbs and sugar. Nine out of ten meals were brown, and a majority of the fruits and vegetables I ate were in the form of processed foods, like French fries.

Fast-forward four years, and I was pushing into a size twenty-eight. I was having panic attacks, depression, night terrors, and anxiety. I'd never experienced any of this before, but it never occurred to me that my diet was the reason I was suffering.

I didn't realize that due to my vegetarianism, I was not getting enough vitamin B12 or the omega-3 fatty acids eicosapentaenoic acid and docosahexaenoic acid. Only after five more years of anxiety, depression, and panic attacks did I come across the Weston A. Price Foundation, which opened my eyes. Cofounded by Sally Fallon Morell and Mary Enig, it's a nonprofit organization committed to bringing nutrient-dense foods back to the human diet. The diet principles they share are based on the fieldwork done in the 1930s and '40s by Weston A. Price, a dentist from Cleveland, Ohio, who studied the health of preindustrial populations and discovered the importance of the fat-soluble vitamins A, D, and K in maintaining the robust health of these cultures. These vitamins are found only in certain seafood, organ meats, and the fats of grass-fed animals.

Ironically, I was a raw vegan when I stumbled across the Weston A. Price Foundation website. After spending hours browsing the site, I decided to start eating meat again. My first taste of bacon was, well, not great. I stayed with it, though, and started adding bone broths and cod liver oil to my diet. I finally was finding some relief from my health problems, but a year later I discovered I had prediabetes and turned again to the Web for more information on diet and health. That's when I found the website *Mark's Daily Apple*, and I made the decision to give up all grains and sugar and follow the Paleo diet. For the first time in years, my brain was humming with happiness. I was eating loads of fat, protein, and veggies and losing weight. My blood sugar was normal, and most of my health issues disappeared.

When my husband saw how much my health improved, he also started following the Paleo diet. For years he had suffered from horrible heartburn and gastroesophageal reflux disease (GERD). He would wake up sick every night. At the time, we both thought this was a normal part of aging. He started following Paleo by simply avoiding grains at dinner, and after a week of that he was sleeping through the night and seeing a huge improvement in his GERD. He started following a full Paleo diet within a month, and a few months after that he'd easily lost thirty pounds.

Despite the improvements to my health, I missed cookies. I missed ice cream! But the few times I

went off the diet and ate "normal" sweets, I found myself experiencing panic attacks. I will never forget the time I ate a cupcake at my niece's birthday party. An hour later I was a wreck, and for the first time I realized how damaging sugar was to my mental health. This was also the first time the phrase "you are what you eat" made sense to me. Until then, I had seen food as completely separate from my health. I mean, yes, I knew that food is fuel, but I didn't understand that my very thoughts and emotions were influenced by the food I was eating! It was a breakthrough moment for me, and I knew I would never go back to the way I used to eat. I would never trade my health and sanity for a cupcake, no matter how good it tastes.

It's a challenge, though, because, I have a solid-gold sweet tooth, and I can't imagine life without my favorite treats. I went online to see if I could find recipes for treats that I could enjoy without the huge sugar spike. After discovering Paleo food blogs, I started tinkering in the kitchen to re-create the comfort foods that called to me from the past.

And there is a *lot* of food calling to me from the past. I tied on my apron when I was eleven and have been in the kitchen ever since. My mother is a taskmaster, no joke, and I can still hear her berating me for the size of my diced onions. I'm thankful to have learned from such an amazing cook. I developed my palate on my mother's handed-down Filipino recipes and my father's traditional Southern foods. When you add in the fact that I'm also a military brat who has lived in Australia, Portugal, and the Philippines, you could say that I've got well-traveled taste buds.

Because I come from people who love to eat, I suppose it's not surprising that most of my favorite family memories are centered on food. With this book and my website, *A Girl Worth Saving*, I hope to help you create new memories around the dinner table and on special occasions, all while promoting healing through diet.

Like most of us, I am not a Paleo perfectionist. I am just a mom who wants to watch her kiddo blow out the candles on his birthday cake every year. This book is about Paleo cooking from the heart.

Blessings!
Kelly Bejelly

Tackling the Paleo Lifestyle

We all know that eating processed foods and sugary treats every day does not constitute a healthy lifestyle. My purpose in creating this book is to provide you with the tools to make three square, Paleo-friendly meals throughout the day, along with healthy, grain-free treats that will prevent you from ending up with a glazed-donut hangover. It's best not to think of Paleo as a one-size-fits-all diet. We're all unique, and our diets should be, too. If you want to eat dairy, do it. (I do.) Want to eat low-carb? Go for it! The important thing is to stick to real, whole, unprocessed foods and avoid anything that causes inflammation in your body.

So now that you're ready to tackle the diet, how should you make the transition? You could try going cold turkey, but for me, the habits that become a permanent part of my lifestyle are the ones that develop slowly over time. But whether you make the transition slowly or overnight, here are some tips for transforming your pantry and health.

1. Remove all processed foods. Reading food labels is a huge wake-up call. Let's compare my recipe for homemade mayo (page 30), which has six easily recognizable ingredients, with store-bought fat-free mayo, which has twenty-six ingredients. The next time you're cooking up something for your family, ask them how they like their Blue 1 or cellulose gel. These ingredients are not food, and you need to remove them from your kitchen and your life. Clear out your pantry and donate the unopened food boxes and canned goods that you will no longer be eating.

2. Move away from grains slowly. When I heard about the carb flu, a two- to three-week period of brain fog and fatigue that comes with an abrupt transition to a low-carb diet, I didn't want anything to with it. I started my journey by eating only soaked and properly fermented grains. After two months of that, I limited my grains to just a piece of soaked bread with lunch. Within four months, I was completely off grains and legumes. Success, and without the carb flu!

3. Stick to the basics. Some of the ingredients for Paleo-friendly meals can be pricey. Focus your spending on the basics: high-quality fats and meats, local and/or organic produce, and nuts and seeds. Limit homemade treats and breads, as those ingredients can pinch your budget. Almond flour and coconut flour arc much more expensive than wheat flour, so the costs of baking really add up.

4. Buy what you can afford. If you have a tight budget, you can still eat amazing foods on this diet. Here are several ways to save money:

- If you can't afford pastured meats, try eating less meat, or simply buy the leanest cuts of meat you can and supplement them with a high-quality fat like coconut oil.

- Eat more pastured eggs. Packed with protein, eggs give you the best nutritional bang for your buck.

- Join or create a food buying club, or shop at a food co-op where you can buy in bulk. Food co-ops charge a minimal markup, and often you get discounts if you volunteer your time, which can help cut your food costs.

- Eat in-season produce.

- Eat more fat. Fat is filling as heck, so you will eat less.

- Stock up on seasonal produce at farmers markets and freeze it to eat during the winter.

- Grow your own food.

- Shop at discount grocery stores and stock up during sales.

- Shop online at Amazon, which has great Subscribe & Save deals on a lot of Paleo-friendly products.

- Prepare basic foods from scratch—bone broth, nut butters, coconut milk, ghee, lard, and so on.

- Buy meat in bulk. Buying half a cow or pig is a big investment up front, but it's the most cost-effective way to get pastured meat in your diet.

- Search Craigslist for small farmers in your area and buy directly from them.

- Check the bulletin board at your local feed store for farmers selling pastured meat. I found a farmer who sells single cuts of grass-fed beef for $5 a pound.

5. Forgive yourself for cheating. Sometimes you may cheat on your diet. Don't be too hard on yourself. It's a journey. Pick yourself up and start again. More than likely, though, you will have some sort of physical reaction to the forbidden food. The first time I ate a "normal" cupcake after going Paleo, I had a terrible panic attack followed by night terrors. I haven't had the inclination to eat "normal" sweets since, especially now that I know how easy it is to whip up a grain-free version that will satisfy my sweet tooth.

What to Eat?

ANIMAL PROTEIN

The best animal protein comes from animals that are raised on their natural diet (not grains!) and allowed to roam freely in the sunshine. Also, make sure to purchase sustainable seafood to keep the oceans healthy.

- Beef
- Buffalo/bison
- Goat
- Lamb
- Pork
- Chicken
- Turkey
- Elk
- Rabbit
- Venison
- Eggs (chicken, duck, or goose)
- Organ meats
- Clams
- Lobster
- Salmon
- Shrimp

VEGETABLES

You can eat your fill of vegetables on the Paleo diet, including sweet potatoes. Organic is best. Local is also great. Every year the Environmental Working Group (ewg.org) puts out the Clean 15 list, which identifies produce that has little to no traces of pesticides, and the Dirty Dozen list, which identifies produce that has been tested for at least 47 different chemicals and has come up positive. If you can't afford to buy all organic, try to buy organic produce from the Dirty Dozen list.

2014 Clean 15

Asparagus, avocados, cabbage, cantaloupe, cauliflower, eggplant, frozen sweet peas, grapefruit, kiwis, mangoes, onions, papayas, pineapples, sweet corn, sweet potatoes

2014 Dirty Dozen

Apples, celery, cherry tomatoes, cucumbers, grapes, imported nectarines, imported snap peas, peaches, potatoes, spinach, strawberries, sweet bell peppers

Suggested veggies

- Acorn squash
- Asparagus
- Artichokes
- Avocados
- Bell peppers
- Broccoli
- Butternut squash
- Carrots
- Cauliflower
- Celery
- Collard greens
- Cucumbers
- Eggplant
- Fennel
- Green onions
- Jicama
- Kale
- Leeks
- Lettuce
- Mushrooms
- Sweet potatoes
- Spinach
- Tomatoes
- Zucchini

HEALTHY FATS

Like me, you probably grew up hearing that saturated fats are bad for you. Thankfully, that lie has been debunked. It turns out that eating naturally occurring fats is healthy. However, some fats are better for specific cooking techniques, as noted below.

Cooking oils for frying and other high-heat uses

- Bacon fat
- Coconut oil
- Beef tallow
- Duck fat
- Lard

Cooking oils for low-heat and nonheat uses

- Avocado oil
- Extra-virgin olive oil
- Macadamia oil
- Sesame oil (untoasted, expeller-pressed)

FRUITS

You can enjoy a multitude of fruits on the Paleo diet. However, if you have blood sugar issues, try to limit your consumption of fruit.

Suggested fruits

- Apples
- Bananas
- Berries (blackberries, blueberries, gooseberries, raspberries, strawberries)
- Cherries
- Coconut
- Grapefruit
- Grapes
- Kiwi
- Lemons
- Limes
- Oranges
- Pears
- Papayas
- Plantains
- Pomegranates
- Stone fruits (apricots, nectarines, peaches)
- Star fruit
- Watermelon

NUTS & SEEDS

Low in carbs and the perfect snack, the following nuts and seeds are allowed on the Paleo diet. However, if you're trying to lose weight, minimize nuts in your diet.

Suggested nuts and seeds

- Almonds
- Cashews
- Hazelnuts
- Macadamia nuts
- Pecans
- Pine nuts
- Walnuts
- Pumpkin seeds
- Sesame seeds
- Sunflower seeds

What to Avoid

GRAINS

The grains you find in today's supermarkets are completely different from the ancient grains of the past. They've been modified to have more gluten, which has been shown to be damaging to the gut.

LEGUMES

I cried big baby tears when I realized that peanuts are legumes, but there are good reasons to avoid them. One, they contain phytates and lectins, which make them hard to digest. Two, they have been shown to lead to leaky gut syndrome, which means the intestinal lining is allowing food particles to pass through and cause any number of problems, such as anxiety, *Candida,* polycystic ovary syndrome, irritable bowel syndrome, and Hashimoto's disease.

Legumes to avoid

- Black beans
- Chickpeas
- Fava beans
- Green and yellow split peas
- Kidney beans
- Lentils
- Lima beans
- Mung beans
- Peanuts
- Pinto beans
- Red beans
- Split peas
- Wax beans

SOY

Traditional cultures did not eat soy that was not properly fermented. Soy has high levels of goitrogens, phytic acid, and phytoestrogens. It should be avoided at all costs, which is often hard to do since it's found in most of the packaged foods for sale in the grocery store. Even good chocolate has soy lecithin in it.

PROCESSED FOODS

Processed foods are filled with a multitude of chemicals and artificial ingredients. Stay away from them.

REFINED SUGAR

White sugar is 99.9 percent sucrose and depletes the body's vitamin B stores. It also has some gnarly affects on the nervous system. You don't have time for that.

The Paleo Pantry

If you're new to the Paleo diet, there are lots of ingredients that you might not be familiar with. Here's an overview.

NONDAIRY MILKS

Almond milk and other nut milks. Made by soaking, grinding, and finally straining nuts, nut milks are common in Paleo dishes, although I prefer coconut milk in my recipes.

Coconut milk. Made from the grated meat of coconuts and water, coconut milk is high in saturated fat. If you buy canned coconut milk, make sure that the cans are BPA-free. Most brands contain guar gum, which some people can't tolerate. Be sure to shake the can well before opening. Refrigerate any leftovers and use within the next two to three days, since it spoils easily. While you can make your own coconut milk (page 34), sometimes I call for canned coconut milk to help create a rich, creamy texture in the dish. I use the Natural Value brand.

FLOURS & MEAL

Almond flour (blanched & superfine). When it comes to creating a light texture in baked goods, nothing beats superfine almond flour. There's a noticeable difference in texture between baked goods made with superfine almond flour and those made with standard almond flour. Superfine almond flour is great for breads, cookies, coating for fried or baked foods, waffles, and pancakes. Made from finely ground blanched almonds, it is high in protein and low in carbs and sugar, and it has a delicate almond flavor that enhances baked goods. Store this flour in your freezer to help extend its shelf life. When measuring this flour, I use the scoop-and-swoop method: dip your measuring cup in the flour and then run a knife across the top of the cup to level it. I recommend the Wellbee's and JK Gourmet brands.

Almond meal. This can be made from whole or blanched almonds, and it's much grittier than almond flour, closer in texture to cornmeal. I rarely use this flour unless I am trying to re-create something that needs a rougher mouth feel. I use Bob's Red Mill brand.

Coconut flour. This flour is made from the coconut meat left over after the milk is extracted. You can make your own coconut flour by grinding up the remaining coconut shreds after making homemade coconut milk, but it's a pretty labor-intensive project. Protein-rich and high in fiber and manganese, this low-carb flour is a moisture-loving beast. It's extremely filling and a great flour alterative for those with nut allergies. It does not perform the same way as wheat flour in recipes, though, and you actually need to use less coconut flour to get the same results. It is excellent in cakes, brownies, pancakes, and muffins, and as a light coating for fried and baked foods. It's also a great filler in dishes like meatloaf and meatballs. The best way to measure coconut flour is the scoop-and-swoop method: dip your measuring cup in the flour and then run a knife across the top of the cup to level it. Coconut flour has the tendency to clump, so sift it after measuring and before adding it to recipes. I buy Tropical Traditions coconut flour.

BAKING INGREDIENTS

Tapioca flour. This high-carb flour is extracted from the cassava or manioc plant. I use it to thicken sauces, and it makes some of the most amazing, breadlike baked goods—it helps bind gluten-free baked goods together and gives them a chewy texture. It's great in breads, pie crusts, shortbread cookies, tortillas, wraps, and batters for deep-frying. It also does not curdle or congeal when refrigerated or frozen. Again, I recommend the scoop-and-swoop method: dip your measuring cup in the flour and then run a knife across the top to level it. I only use the Bob's Red Mill brand.

Baking powder (gluten-free). Baking powder is a combination of baking soda, cream of tartar, and a "moisture-absorbing agent" that is quite often wheat starch. Make sure to purchase a gluten-free version to avoid this.

Baking soda. This is just plain sodium bicarbonate, and it helps give baked goods a little lift.

Cacao powder. Made from finely ground raw cacao beans, this unsweetened powder contains an abundance of magnesium and iron, which is a good reason to enjoy a spoonful in your smoothies every day. I buy Navitas Naturals brand.

Chocolate bars (baking, unsweetened). Made exclusively from unsweetened cacao, these are great for making your own soy-free chocolate or for packing an extra-powerful chocolate flavor into baked goods. I use the organic, fair-trade, 100 percent cacao baking bar from Sunspire.

Chocolate chips, bittersweet (70% cacao). Vegan, soy-free, and gluten-free, these make a quick treat and are a must-have for chocolate chip cookies. I use Equal Exchange's semisweet chocolate chips.

Coconut butter. This is basically puréed coconut meat, and it works great as a spread or in baking as a replacement for almond butter. It does solidify in cold weather, so warm it up in a warm water bath before mixing together the separated coconut oil and coconut meat. You can easily make coconut butter at home by placing 8 ounces of unsweetened shredded coconut in your blender with 1 tablespoon of coconut oil. Blend on high until smooth. If you buy it, I recommend Artisana's brand.

Dates (Deglet Noor). Also known as the Date of Light, the Deglet Noor is lightly sweet and nutty. These dates have a firmer texture than most dates. They keep well and are low in moisture, so you don't have to refrigerate them. These are the only dates I keep in my pantry. When I use them in recipes, I simply chop them in my food processor with the other ingredients so that they are well incorporated. You can soak them, but I usually forget to plan ahead, and my food processor makes easy work of breaking the dates down. They give a delicious buttery flavor to baked goods, and I love using them as an alternative sweetener in cookie recipes.

Gelatin. By using gelatin, you can make amazing "cream" pies without a drop of dairy. It also supports skin, hair, and nail growth and improves digestion. You can't go wrong with this amazing food. I only use Great Lakes brand unflavored beef gelatin, in the red can.

Apple butter. This is essentially a concentrated form of applesauce. It's made by slow-cooking apples with cider or water until they caramelize and turn dark brown. I like to use apple butter in coconut flour–based recipes to provide moisture and help reduce the number of eggs needed. I like Eden Foods Organic Apple Butter.

Pumpkin pie spice. This spice mixture contains ground cinnamon, nutmeg, ginger, and allspice. I like to use it in cakes and cookies because it's easier than measuring each individual spice.

SWEETENERS

Blackstrap molasses. This is the dark, thick syrup created during the extraction of raw cane sugar. Unlike refined sugars, it contains vitamin B6, calcium, magnesium, iron, and manganese. It's also a great source of potassium and adds a rich, bittersweet flavor to dishes.

Coconut sugar. Made from the "sap" of coconut flowers, this sugar gives a delicious caramel flavor to recipes. Reputed to be a lower glycemic sweetener, it can be substituted 1:1 for granulated sugar.

Honey (raw). Honey is a powerful antibacterial substance that contains vitamins B2, B3, B5, and C. It's sweeter than maple syrup and easier to digest because it's mostly made up of simple sugars. I rarely use honey in baking, but some recipes just require that delicate sweet flavor to taste right.

Maple syrup (Grade B). This is my favorite sweetener for desserts and the one used most frequently in this book. It's darker in color and less refined than Grade A, so it does retain some minerals, and it has the most delicious caramel undertones. Surprisingly, it has less sugar than honey.

FATS & OILS

Bacon fat. This is a delicious and healthy fat, so be sure to save the drippings after you cook up a batch of bacon. Simply pour the warm liquid through a strainer into a wide-mouth glass canning jar and cover with a lid. You can keep bacon fat on your countertop for four months, in the fridge for six months, or in the freezer for one year.

Coconut oil. I prefer expeller-pressed coconut oil, which is extracted mechanically, not by solvents. It has almost no coconut flavor and yet you still get all of the benefits of medium-chain fatty acids, such as lauric acid. I use the Tropical Traditions brand.

Lard. Lard is pig fat, and the highest grade comes from around the animal's kidneys and inside the loin. It is best to use lard from a farm-raised animal that has not been treated with antibiotics because fat holds the body's toxins. Lard has a high smoke point, and chefs consider it superior to shortening. I recommend purchasing lard from the Fatworks Foods or U.S. Wellness Meats.

Palm shortening. I love palm shortening for frosting and baked goods. To me, it's like a dairy-free version of butter. I only use Tropical Traditions brand, which comes from small farms that meet strict social and environmental criteria.

KEY SEASONINGS & FLAVORINGS

Apple cider vinegar. Look for a brand that is unheated, unfiltered, and unpasteurized. I love the sweet, zesty taste of apples that apple cider vinegar adds to dishes. I use Bragg's brand.

Coconut aminos. Made from the mineral-rich "sap" of coconut blossoms, coconut aminos are packed full of amino acids and minerals. Coconut aminos are the perfect replacement for soy sauce.

Fish sauce. Fish sauce packs a punch of flavor and is a must-have for any Asian cuisine recipe. I use Red Boat brand because it's minimally processed and made with sea salt and wild black anchovies.

Sea salt (fine). I use finely ground sea salt in all the recipes in this book. Sea salt gives a great flavor to dishes and provides the added bonus of minerals, such as calcium, magnesium, copper, and iron. You will find you need to add less sea salt to recipes to get the same great flavor. My go-to sea salt is the extra-fine dark pink Himalayan salt from The Spice Lab.

Worcestershire sauce. This fermented condiment adds a meaty flavor to recipes. It's typically used when making beef jerky, but I think it's also a must-have for Salisbury steak. I use The Wizard's Organic Gluten-free Worcestershire Sauce, which does have tamari in it. You can easily swap this out for fish sauce.

MISCELLANEOUS FAVORITES

Plantain chips. Crispy plantain chips fried in palm oil make a great snack and work wonderfully as breading. I use Inka Chips brand.

Pork rinds. Made from the skin of the pig and a by-product of rendering lard, you'll either love or hate these crispy delicacies. I love to use them as breading for chicken or as filler in meatballs and meatloaf. I buy mine from U.S. Wellness Meats.

Tools for the Paleo Kitchen

Now that you've stocked your panty, let's make sure you have the tools you need to whip up all those tasty recipes. The good news is that you'll need fewer gadgets than you might suppose, so you can invest in higher-end products that will make your prep time so much easier.

Blender. A professional blender will change your life in the kitchen. I can't tell you how many times I've tried to get a mixture smooth but my food processor wasn't cutting it. Now I pop the mixture in my Blendtec blender, and it becomes smooth and silky. You can also use a blender to grind nut flours and make soups, smoothies, ice creams, and more. I use mine every day and love that it comes with a BPA-free carafe.

Cast-iron pans. I adore cast-iron pans; I cook most of our meals in my trusty 15-inch Lodge skillet. You can't go wrong with one of these inexpensive and durable pans in your cupboard. Just make sure the pan is seasoned before you use it, and take care when cleaning it (see page 21). If you can swing the cost, buy Le Creuset enameled cast-iron pans. They make for easy cleanup and last forever.

Food processor. I would be lost without my Cuisinart food processor. Invest in a good one to chop, rice, shred, dice, purée, and more without using any elbow grease. This is another machine I use every day, and you will find that I reference it often in the recipes in this book.

Knives. I never knew what I was missing until I got a good set of knives. Honestly, you shouldn't have to saw through a tomato for 10 minutes. I only really use three knives: a 7-inch Santoku knife, a paring knife, and a 6-inch serrated knife.

Ice cream maker. Who doesn't like ice cream? I have never met a single person who turns up their nose at it. One of the best reasons to invest in an ice cream maker is that you can control the ingredients in your ice cream, as well as how much sugar goes into it. Plus, there's the added bonus of being able to lick the paddle after making a fresh batch. I use a Cuisinart ice cream maker.

Silicone baking mat and parchment paper. There is no baking or candy making without these two products. A silicone baking mat is reusable and makes any surface nonstick. I have noticed that baking times need to be adjusted with a silicone baking mat; it often makes baked goods softer. I use the Silpat brand of silicone baking mats.

I use parchment paper to make rolling out sticky dough easier. I also line my baking sheets with it to make cleanup a breeze. Cookies that are baked on a parchment paper–lined baking sheet don't spread as much as those baked directly on the baking sheet.

Spiral slicer. If you miss pasta noodles, you need one of these tools in your life. (The most popular brand is Spiralizer.) Equipped with three different blades, it can turn a variety of vegetables into skinny noodles similar to spaghetti noodles, thicker noodles similar to curly fries, and ribbon noodles. From butternut squash to pears, the noodle options are endless. My absolute favorites are sweet potato noodles crisped up in the oven.

HOW TO SEASON AND CLEAN A CAST-IRON SKILLET

Did you just buy an unseasoned cast-iron skillet? Are you starting to see dull or rusty spots, or finding that food keeps getting stuck during cooking? If so, it's time to season your cast-iron pan.

What You Need:
- Cast-iron skillet
- Dish soap
- Stiff brush
- Clean, dry cloth
- Coconut oil

1. Preheat the oven to 325°F.
2. Wash the skillet with warm, soapy water and a stiff brush. Please note that cast iron normally should not be washed with soap, but it's fine here since the pan is about to be seasoned.
3. Rinse and thoroughly dry the skillet.
4. Using a cloth, apply a thin coat of coconut oil to the inside and outside of the skillet.
5. Place the skillet on the oven's center rack. Place a rimmed baking sheet underneath the rack to catch any drips.
6. Bake for 1 hour.
7. Turn off the heat and allow to the skillet to cool completely before removing it from the oven.

After using your cast-iron skillet, don't use soap to clean it. Here's what to do instead:

1. Clean the skillet immediately after use, while it is still warm. Don't soak the pan or it may rust.
2. Wash it by hand using hot water and a stiff brush to remove any food particles.
3. To remove stubborn food residue, use boiling water or scrub the pan with coarse kosher salt.
4. Dry it thoroughly with a dish towel.
5. With a cloth, apply a light coating of coconut oil over the bottom and sides of the pan. Buff off any excess oil.
6. Store the skillet in a dry place.

Slow cooker. As labor-intensive as the Paleo diet is, there are times when you a need break. A slow cooker is a lazy cook's must-have tool. I own two, and you can make everything from breakfast to dessert in one of these gadgets.

Spatulas (heat-resistant). I would be lost without these; I use them 90 percent of the time when mixing up something in my kitchen.

Meat thermometer. These gadgets are really inexpensive and will help you be certain that the foods you are about to eat are not undercooked. Trust me, there is nothing worse than biting into a piece of fried chicken that is cold and rare inside. Just the visual is enough to give me the heebie-jeebies. Buy a thermometer today!

How to Use This Book

This book is packed with some of my absolute favorite comfort foods made Paleo-friendly, from Southern to Mediterranean to Filipino dishes (thanks, Mom!). You'll find the perfect recipe to make dinner a success for you and your kids, even the picky eaters.

You will find breads, soups, salads, main courses, sides, and irresistible desserts that are the perfect indulgence. I hope that you enjoy my recipes and that they soon become your favorites, too. And once you've familiarized yourself with Paleo ingredients (especially the gluten-free flours, which are often a stumbling block when transitioning to Paleo), I hope that you experiment and create your own original treats or re-create old family favorites, especially those passed-down holiday cookies. I'd love to hear how your kitchen experimentation turns out, so email me. (You can find my contact info on my website, *A Girl Worth Saving.*)

To help you Paleo-fy your favorite baking recipes and make the transition to working with gluten-free flours as smooth as possible, I've included a detailed tutorial called "Kelly's Paleo Baking Tutorial" on pages 274 to 279.

In the back of the book, you will find sections on conversions, equivalents, substitutions, and a glossary of basic cooking terms, all designed to help make your kitchen experiments successful.

Before You Begin

Here are seven important tips for getting successful results in the kitchen:

1. Read through the recipe from start to finish to make sure you understand each step. A couple of recipes require some attention when they are almost finished. Reading through the recipe before starting to cook ensures that you won't be blindsided by "surprise" steps.

2. Check out the information about gluten-free flours on page 16 and in "Kelly's Paleo Baking Tutorial" (pages 274 to 279). These sections include some important tips on how to work with each flour. Tapioca flour, in particular, can be difficult to work with, so please be sure to read about it before using it.

3. All of the flour measurements in this book are based on using the scoop-and-swoop method: I dip my measuring cup into the canister to fill it and use the flat edge of a knife to swoop the excess, making the flour level with the top of the measuring cup.

4. To get an accurate measurement of liquid sweeteners, lightly grease the measuring spoon or cup before pouring.

5. Some of my recipes call for canned, full-fat coconut milk while others call for homemade coconut milk. This is because some dishes need the fat content of canned coconut milk to turn out correctly. When I call for homemade coconut milk, I do not want the recipe to have a strong coconut flavor.

6. I have created special categories to help you find recipes for specific occasions or diet plans. Keep an eye out for the following tags: Birthday, Valentine's Day, Game Day, Holiday (Thanksgiving and Christmas), and AIP.

Birthday *Valentine's Day* *Game day* *Holiday* AIP

7. Whenever eggs aren't cooked in a recipe, I specifically call for pastured eggs. Eggs from chickens raised in spacious, clean coops with access to sunlight and the ability to forage have a much lower risk of testing positive for salmonella. I prefer to err on the side of caution, and I always use pastured eggs whenever I am eating raw eggs.

AIP. If you have an autoimmune condition, your immune system mistakenly attacks your own body instead of attacking foreign invaders. The Autoimmune Protocol (AIP) helps your body recover by removing foods that cause inflammation. Of course, there's more to managing an autoimmune condition than just avoiding certain foods—managing stress, getting good sleep, exercising, and, in some cases, taking medication are all important—but your diet is a great place to start.

DIET

Recipes in this book that are AIP-friendly are marked with an icon: . If you're interested in learning more, please check out the AIP resources on page 284.

Ready? Tie those apron strings and have fun! Cooking is a constant adventure, with tons of variables to keep you on your toes. You'll never get bored!

CHAPTER 1

THE BASICS

Barbecue Sauce

I can't remember a summer growing up when we didn't have the grill going full blast. My mother is famous for her barbecue sauce; she even bottled and sold it at one time. When I went Paleo, I knew that I had to try to re-create it for my family. After removing three-quarters of the sugar from her recipe, adding bacon fat for a nice smoky taste, and substituting natural sweeteners for the granulated sugar, I came up with this winner. You will want to smother your grilled foods in this sauce and lick every bit of it off your fingers.

PREP TIME
5 min

COOK TIME
30 min

MAKES
1½ cups

INGREDIENTS

1 cup water

1 (6-ounce) can tomato paste

¼ cup apple cider vinegar

¼ cup maple syrup

3 tablespoons bacon fat

2 tablespoons blackstrap molasses

2 teaspoons garlic powder

1 teaspoon red pepper flakes

½ teaspoon sea salt

¼ teaspoon ground black pepper

1. In a saucepan, whisk together the water, tomato paste, vinegar, maple syrup, bacon fat, and molasses.

2. Whisk in the garlic powder, red pepper flakes, salt, and pepper. Cook for 30 minutes on low.

Ketchup

The sweet and tangy ketchup is a must when eating hot dogs, hamburgers, eggs, and Sweet Potato Fries (page 212). My favorite way to eat it is hot out of the pan! I highly recommend trying it that way, as most people never experience the magical taste of hot ketchup. The flavor is excellent when chilled, too. In fact, it only gets better as it ages in the refrigerator, but this ketchup never lasts long in my house. You can easily punch up the heat by adding more cayenne pepper.

PREP TIME	COOK TIME	MAKES
5 min	20 min	2 cups

INGREDIENTS

1 (6-ounce) can tomato paste

1 (14-ounce) can diced tomatoes, no added salt, drained

½ cup water

2 tablespoons apple cider vinegar

3 tablespoons honey

½ teaspoon sea salt

½ teaspoon onion powder

½ teaspoon ground allspice

¼ teaspoon cayenne pepper

1. In a blender, combine the tomato paste, diced tomatoes, water, vinegar, and honey and blend until completely smooth, approximately 1 minute. Add the salt, onion powder, allspice, and cayenne pepper and blend for 30 seconds.

2. Pour the mixture into a small saucepan and bring to a boil. Lower the heat to medium-low and simmer for 20 minutes.

3. Let cool, then pour into a jar and store in the refrigerator. It will keep for about 3 weeks.

Homemade Mayo

Homemade mayonnaise is the bee's knees. It's also simple to make, and once you've done it, you will be hooked. You can make mayo with any light-flavored oil, such as walnut oil, avocado oil, or grapeseed oil. Every oil has a unique flavor, so experiment and find the one you like best. You can also add an array of spices and ingredients to jazz up this condiment (see Variations, below).

PREP TIME

5 min

MAKES
1½ cups

INGREDIENTS

2 large egg yolks

1 tablespoon lemon juice

1 tablespoon apple cider vinegar

1 teaspoon honey

½ teaspoon sea salt

1½ cups light olive oil

1. In a blender, combine the egg yolks, lemon juice, vinegar, honey, and salt. Turn the blender on low and slowly drizzle in the olive oil. Continue until all of the oil is gone and then blend until the mayo has a thick, creamy consistency.

2. Transfer the mayo to a jar and refrigerate. It will last up to a week in the refrigerator.

VARIATIONS: Adding spices will kick your mayo up a notch. Try garlic powder or fresh minced garlic to transform the mayo into an aioli. Dried dill weed, chopped sun-dried tomatoes, chopped fresh basil, or chopped chipotle pepper are also great.

NOTE: If the mayo fails to emulsify, set it in the refrigerator for 2 hours—it thickens as it chills. Then simply stir with a wire whisk to combine. It will be runnier than regular mayo, though, and more suitable for salad dressings.

Sweet-and-Sour Sauce

Tomatoes, pineapple, and garlic marry to create this well-loved sauce that's tart, savory, and sweet all at the same time. If you make this sauce ahead of time, it's easy to pull together a quick meal of sweet-and-sour pork or chicken on those nights when you just don't want to cook. Used as a dipping sauce, it's a fantastic way to jazz up chicken nuggets; my son requests it constantly. Whatever you do, don't omit the pineapple. It's the secret ingredient that really makes this sauce.

PREP TIME
15 min

COOK TIME
35 min

MAKES
2 cups

INGREDIENTS

1 tablespoon coconut oil

1 small yellow onion, diced

2 cloves garlic, minced

1 cup Chicken Bone Broth (page 44)

¼ cup tomato paste

1 (8-ounce) can crushed pineapple, with juice

3 tablespoons maple syrup

1 tablespoon coconut aminos

½ teaspoon sea salt

¼ teaspoon ground black pepper

1. Place the coconut oil, onion, and garlic in a saucepan over medium heat. Cook until the onion is translucent, about 5 minutes.

2. Add the remaining ingredients and mix with a spoon until well combined. Cook for 30 minutes.

3. Pour into a blender and purée until smooth. Let cool, then transfer to a glass jar and store in the refrigerator. This sauce will keep for approximately a week.

Coconut Milk

I personally do not like the taste of canned, full-fat coconut milk in drinks or smoothies. Making coconut milk from scratch is simple and inexpensive, and it gives you the perfect, light-tasting coconut milk for beverages or to pour over cereal. If you're feeling adventurous, you can use the leftover shredded coconut to make coconut flour (see below).

PREP TIME   COOK TIME   MAKES

 5 min   5 min   2 cups

INGREDIENTS

1 cup unsweetened shredded coconut

2 cups boiling water

¼ teaspoon sea salt

DIET

 AIP

NOTE: When coconut milk is chilled, the fat separates from the milk. You can skim it from the top and use it in any recipe that calls for coconut oil. Shake the rest of the mixture to combine, and use it in place of milk.

TIP: A paint strainer bag from your local hardware store makes an inexpensive nut milk bag.

VARIATION: For "buttermilk," add 1 tablespoon of lemon juice or apple cider vinegar and whisk to combine.

1. In a blender, combine the shredded coconut, boiling water, and salt and blend on high for 1 minute.

2. Strain the mixture through a nut milk bag into a heatproof glass jar and let cool. (Save the shredded coconut for homemade coconut flour; see below.)

3. Once cool, store in the refrigerator (see Note). The milk will keep for 3 days.

HOW TO MAKE COCONUT FLOUR

1. Preheat the oven to 170°F.

2. Place the shredded coconut left over from 1 batch of coconut milk in a thin layer on a rimmed baking sheet. Bake for 40 to 45 minutes, until it is completely dry to the touch.

3. Place the dried shredded coconut in a food processor and pulse for 1 to 2 minutes, until you have a fine flour. Store in an airtight jar in the refrigerator. It will keep for 4 to 5 months.

Teriyaki Sauce

If you've been missing the thick, sweet teriyaki sauce that you used to enjoy in your pre-Paleo days, now you can have it again. Get creative with this quick, simple sauce: put it over chicken wings or burgers, use it to marinate salmon, or enjoy it as a dipping sauce for Chicken Katsu (page 124) or Sweet Potato Fries (page 212).

PREP TIME   COOK TIME   MAKES

 5 min   2 min   1 cup

INGREDIENTS

½ cup coconut aminos

¼ cup water

2 tablespoons honey

1 tablespoon apple cider vinegar

½ teaspoon ginger powder

½ teaspoon garlic powder

1 teaspoon tapioca flour

DIET

 AIP

1. In a saucepan off the heat, whisk together all of the ingredients.

2. Set the pan over medium-high heat and cook, whisking constantly, for about 2 minutes, or until the sauce thickens.

3. Remove from the heat and let cool before transferring to a jar. The sauce will keep in the refrigerator for up to 2 weeks.

Ranch Dressing

Considering that ranch is one of the most popular salad dressings in the United States, it's surprising that I didn't try it until I was in college. When I did try it, though, I fell in love with its zesty flavor and creamy texture, and it didn't take me long to figure out how to make a dairy-free version that matches the texture of the original. The secret ingredients of this re-creation are parsley, Homemade Mayo (page 30), and homemade Coconut Milk (page 34). This dressing is also excellent as a dip for veggies, Bucha Onion Rings (page 184), or Sweet Potato Fries (page 212).

PREP TIME

5 min

plus 2 hours to chill

MAKES

1¼ cups

INGREDIENTS

1 cup Homemade Mayo (page 30)

¼ cup Coconut Milk (page 34)

1 tablespoon dried parsley

½ teaspoon garlic powder

½ teaspoon onion powder

¼ teaspoon ground black pepper

1. Place all of the ingredients in a small bowl and whisk to combine.

2. Transfer to a container and chill for 2 hours before using. It will last for up to a week in the refrigerator.

Honey Mustard

When I first started working on this recipe, I had no idea how spicy dried yellow mustard is. I liken it to napalm. After scorching my taste buds over several attempts, I finally got smarter and used mayo as the base that helps pull this recipe together. If you want it a bit sweeter, you can add more honey, but I love it exactly as it turned out. You can use it on salads, hamburgers, and Chicken Katsu (page 124) or as a dipping sauce for Sweet Potato Fries (page 212).

PREP TIME

5
min

MAKES

¾
cup

INGREDIENTS

½ cup Homemade Mayo (page 30)

2 tablespoons canned, full-fat coconut milk

2 teaspoons dry mustard

1 teaspoon honey

1. Place all of the ingredients in a small bowl and whisk until smooth.

2. Store in an airtight container in the refrigerator. It will keep for about a week.

Tahini Sauce

Garlic, sesame seeds, and cinnamon come together to make a piquant sauce with roots in Mediterranean cuisine. Roasting the sesame seeds brings a new layer of flavor to this sauce, but make sure you watch them the entire time so they don't burn. This sauce livens up simple roasted cauliflower, makes the perfect dip for raw vegetables, and can jazz up any salad. It's also great on Lamb Gyro Burgers (page 140).

PREP TIME   COOK TIME   MAKES

5 min   8 min   2 cups

INGREDIENTS

1 cup raw sesame seeds

3 cloves garlic, minced

2 tablespoons minced fresh curly parsley

2 tablespoons lemon juice

½ teaspoon ground cinnamon

½ teaspoon sea salt

¾ cup extra-virgin olive oil

½ cup water

1. In a stainless-steel skillet over medium-low heat, roast the sesame seeds for 5 to 8 minutes, gently tossing the seeds in the pan to keep them from darkening. When the seeds are just lightly browned and fragrant, pour them into a food processor. Turn on the machine and grind for 20 seconds.

2. Add the garlic, parsley, lemon juice, cinnamon, and salt to the processor and pulse for 20 seconds.

3. While the machine is running, drizzle in the olive oil and then the water until you have a thick paste. Store in an airtight container in the refrigerator for up to 2 weeks.

NOTE: This sauce may separate in the refrigerator. Simply stir it with a spoon to recombine.

Chicken Bone Broth

Chicken broth is a superfood that's sometimes called Mother Nature's penicillin for its flu-fighting ability. It also helps heal your gut and promotes healthy digestion—especially when you add chicken feet. I won't lie, the first time I put chicken feet in my broth, it was hard to take in the visual without shuddering. However, the gut-healing benefits of the gelatin and minerals in chicken feet can't be beat.

PREP TIME 10 min   COOK TIME 12-18 hours   MAKES 6 cups

INGREDIENTS

1 chicken carcass

2 chicken feet, thoroughly cleaned (see Note)

2 large carrots, cut into large chunks

3 bay leaves

1 stalk celery

30 black peppercorns

1 bunch fresh curly parsley, chopped

1 large yellow onion, halved

2 tablespoons apple cider vinegar

8 cups water

1. Place the chicken carcass, chicken feet, carrots, bay leaves, celery, peppercorns, parsley, onion, and vinegar in a slow cooker. Cover with the water and cook on low for 12 to 18 hours.

2. Strain through a colander or strainer lined with cheesecloth and store in a tightly sealed jar. It will keep for a week in the refrigerator, or you can freeze it in freezer-safe canning jars for later use.

NOTE: Before adding the chicken feet to the slow cooker, make sure they've been cleaned thoroughly and the skin has been removed. Most of the time you will get them already prepared from your farmer, but if not, you will need to clean them yourself: Rub them with salt, scald them briefly in boiling water, and then plunge them into an icy bath. This will make it easy to remove the yellow membranes. Peel the yellow membranes from the feet and chop the talons off at the first knuckle. The chicken feet are now ready to use!

Hot Sauce

Dates give this hot sauce an amazing depth of flavor. This easy recipe creates a tangy and slightly sweet hot sauce with a medium level of heat. I use it liberally on steak and as a dipping sauce for Sweet Potato Fries (page 212).

PREP TIME
COOK TIME
MAKES
20 min
40 min
1½ cups

INGREDIENTS

2 large red bell peppers, seeded and chopped

20 red serrano peppers, seeded and chopped (see Note)

6 cloves garlic, minced

6 whole Deglet Noor dates, pitted

1 cup apple cider vinegar

¼ cup honey

2 tablespoons fish sauce

1 teaspoon sea salt

1. In a well-ventilated area, combine all of the ingredients in a large saucepan and bring to a boil over medium heat.

2. Lower the heat and let simmer for 30 minutes.

3. Pour the ingredients into a blender and pulse until smooth.

4. Let cool and store in a glass jar in the refrigerator. This sauce will keep for about 3 weeks.

NOTE: Make sure to wear disposable gloves while working with the serranos and cook this sauce in well-ventilated area, as the capsaicin in the peppers is released into the air during cooking and can cause inhalation burns.

Pesto

Freshly made pesto trumps the stuff you can buy at the grocery store and is so easy to make. It is also very versatile: You can add it to soups, use it to glam up your scrambled eggs, or use it as a pizza topping. And of course, it's always delicious with Paleo-friendly noodles. One of my favorite meals is a big plate of Zucchini Noodles (page 210) tossed with this pesto and leftover chicken.

PREP TIME 5 min

COOK TIME 4 min

MAKES 1½ cups

INGREDIENTS

¼ cup raw pumpkin seeds

3 cloves garlic, peeled

3 cups lightly packed spinach

1 cup packed fresh basil leaves (about 1 bunch)

1 teaspoon sea salt

¼ teaspoon ground black pepper

¼ teaspoon ground nutmeg

½ cup extra-virgin olive oil

1. In a skillet over medium heat, lightly toast the pumpkin seeds for 4 minutes, or until lightly browned and fragrant.

2. Place the toasted pumpkin seeds and garlic in a food processor and pulse until smooth.

3. Add the spinach, basil, salt, pepper, and nutmeg and turn on the food processor.

4. While the machine is running, slowly drizzle in the olive oil until well combined.

5. Use immediately. Store any leftover sauce in an airtight jar in the refrigerator. It will keep for 3 to 4 days.

Slow Cooker Spaghetti Sauce

The smell of this sauce bubbling away in the slow cooker is divine, and once you taste it, you'll never want to go back to store-bought spaghetti sauce. I make a large batch and freeze it to use for quick, easy meals on those nights when takeout is calling. You can also use this sauce to top Pizza Crust (page 72) or to jazz up Meatloaf (page 122).

PREP TIME COOK TIME MAKES

15 min   6-8 hours   10 cups

INGREDIENTS

2 large portobello mushroom caps, diced

1 large yellow onion, diced

6 cloves garlic, chopped

½ cup chopped fresh Italian parsley

2 (28-ounce) cans diced tomatoes, drained and rinsed

1 (6-ounce) can tomato paste

1 cup Chicken Bone Broth (page 44)

½ cup extra-virgin olive oil

2 teaspoons dried oregano

1 teaspoon dried basil

1 teaspoon sea salt

½ teaspoon dried crushed rosemary

½ teaspoon dried fennel seeds

½ teaspoon red pepper flakes

½ teaspoon ground black pepper

1. Place all of the ingredients in a 6-quart slow cooker and stir well to combine.

2. Cook on the high setting for 6 to 8 hours. The result will be a chunky-style sauce. If you want a smooth sauce, you can purée it in the slow cooker using an immersion blender or purée it in small batches in a regular blender.

3. This sauce will keep for a week in the refrigerator. You can also freeze it in freezer-safe wide-mouth mason jars and reheat as needed.

Thai Almond Sauce

This easy, no-cook sauce has an authentic Thai taste. You would never guess that it's made with almond butter instead of the traditional peanut butter. It is thick, nutty, and rich with spices, and it makes a great dipping sauce for chicken, beef, or pork. The dishes you make with it are limited only by your imagination! I love throwing it in a cast-iron skillet with chicken and serving it over Garlic Fried Rice (page 180). You can also use it as a dipping sauce for Chicken Katsu (page 124) or toss it with Zucchini Noodles (page 210) for a quick meal.

PREP TIME

10 min

MAKES
2¼ cups

INGREDIENTS

1 cup smooth almond butter

1 cup canned, full-fat coconut milk

1 teaspoon fish sauce

2 tablespoons coconut aminos

¼ cup lime juice

½ teaspoon garlic powder

½ teaspoon ginger powder

½ teaspoon ground coriander

1 teaspoon honey (optional)

2 tablespoons dried cilantro leaves

1. Place the almond butter, coconut milk, fish sauce, and coconut aminos in a large bowl and whisk to combine.

2. Add the lime juice, garlic powder, ginger powder, coriander, honey (if using), and cilantro and whisk until smooth.

3. This sauce will keep for up to 2 weeks in the refrigerator. You can also freeze it and reheat later for an easy meal.

Mushroom Gravy

So many dishes taste better with a rich mushroom gravy served over the top. This simple recipe is a must-have for any holiday table. It's flavorful and meaty, and even my husband, an admitted mushroom hater, loves it. It is the perfect sauce to serve over Mashed "Potatoes" (page 178) or Meatloaf (page 122).

PREP TIME 15 min

COOK TIME 20 min

MAKES 2 cups

INGREDIENTS

2 tablespoons coconut oil

1 small yellow onion, diced

1 large portobello mushroom cap, diced

1½ cups Chicken Bone Broth (page 44)

1 teaspoon sea salt

½ teaspoon dried thyme leaves

1 tablespoon tapioca flour

2 tablespoons canned, full-fat coconut milk

DIET **AIP**

OCCASION *Holiday*

1. Combine the coconut oil, onion, and diced mushroom in a skillet over medium heat. Sauté for 3 to 5 minutes, until the onion is translucent.

2. Add the broth, salt, and thyme and bring to a boil. Reduce the heat and let simmer for 10 minutes.

3. In a small bowl, whisk together the tapioca flour and coconut milk. Pour this mixture into the pan and whisk until smooth.

4. Using an immersion blender, blend until smooth. Alternatively, you can transfer the gravy to a blender to blend.

5. Use immediately or freeze for later use. To reheat, first defrost the gravy completely and then pour it into a saucepan over medium heat. Whisk to recombine and warm, about 5 minutes.

Salsa Verde

Tomatillos are small fruits that look like tomatoes with papery coverings or "dresses," as my son likes to say. They have a slightly tart flavor and are the stars in this recipe. My husband puts salsa verde on almost everything—eggs, vegetables—and I think I've even seen him eyeing his pancakes, wondering how it would taste. This recipe adds a slight creaminess from the avocado and just gets better as it ages in the refrigerator.

PREP TIME   COOK TIME   MAKES

20 min   15 min   6 cups

INGREDIENTS

2 pounds tomatillos

1 small yellow onion, quartered

4 cloves garlic, peeled

1 small avocado, halved, pitted, and peeled

1 cup chopped fresh cilantro

1 teaspoon sea salt

½ teaspoon ground black pepper

¼ teaspoon dried oregano leaves

¼ teaspoon ground cumin

1. Peel the papery skins off the tomatillos and place the tomatillos in a large pot. Cover with water and bring to a boil. Reduce the heat to medium and cook for 10 minutes, then drain.

2. Cut the tomatillos in half and place them in a food processor along with the rest of the ingredients. Pulse until smooth.

3. This salsa will keep for up to a week in the refrigerator. You can also freeze small quantities to use later as needed.

Strawberry Jam

I love making jam from scratch. The smell of it bubbling away is just heavenly, and of course I just can't have a biscuit unless it's smothered in something sweet. The strawberries in this recipe can easily be swapped out for blueberries, blackberries, or raspberries. Instead of pectin, I prefer to use gelatin, which adds a host of health benefits in addition to giving the jam a thick consistency. Note that you cannot preserve jams that contain gelatin with a pressure canner or water bath canner; instead, you must freeze them.

PREP TIME	COOK TIME	MAKES
15 min	35 min	1½ cups

plus 5 hours to chill

INGREDIENTS

1 pound fresh strawberries, hulled and quartered

½ cup water

2 tablespoons honey

¼ teaspoon ground cinnamon

½ teaspoon vanilla extract

⅛ teaspoon sea salt

1 tablespoon beef gelatin

DIET

 AIP

1. Place the strawberries, water, honey, cinnamon, vanilla extract, and salt in a saucepan and bring to a boil over medium heat.

2. Reduce the heat to medium-low and cook for 30 minutes. Mash the strawberries with a fork periodically to help break them up.

3. Add the gelatin and whisk for 1 minute to combine.

4. Pour into a clean glass canning jar and replace the lid. Let cool to room temperature, then put in the refrigerator to set for 4 to 5 hours.

5. This jam will keep for up to a week in the refrigerator. You can also freeze it in small freezer-safe jars and defrost as needed.

Powdered Sugar

In my house growing up, powdered sugar was referred to as "candy dust." My mother lightly dusted cakes with it, but I just went at it with a spoon. Whenever you want to pretty up a cake or cookies, make frosting, or tackle homemade macaroons, you'll need powdered sugar, and this super simple recipe delivers. And because it uses coconut sugar instead of refined sugar, this recipe is much healthier than store-bought powdered sugar.

PREP TIME

2 min

MAKES

1 cup

INGREDIENTS

½ cup coconut sugar

½ cup tapioca flour

1. In a small bowl, combine the coconut sugar and tapioca flour. Mix well with a spoon.

2. Pour the mixture into a coffee grinder or spice grinder and pulse until powdered and light in color.

3. Store in an airtight jar for up to 6 months.

Cashew Sour Cream

Cashews can be transformed into great replacements for dairy products because they have a similar buttery taste. After soaking, they are easy to process into a thick sauce, which makes an excellent substitute for dairy-based sour cream.

PREP TIME

5 min

plus 6 hours to soak

MAKES

2 cups

INGREDIENTS

1 cup raw cashews

3 cups water, divided

¼ cup lemon juice

1. Place the cashews in a large bowl and cover with 2 cups of the water. Let soak for 6 hours at room temperature.

2. Drain the cashews and place in a food processor or blender. Add the lemon juice and remaining 1 cup of water and purée until smooth.

3. Store in an airtight container in the refrigerator for up to a week.

CHAPTER 2

BREADS, WRAPS, & PASTRIES

Caramel Apple Cinnamon Rolls

The first time I took a bite of these rolls, I wanted to slap myself, they were so dang good. They are so close to the real deal that tasting them could convert the most ardent grain lovers to the Paleo diet. These rolls make for an indulgent breakfast and an even better dessert.

PREP TIME
20 min

COOK TIME
45 min

MAKES
6 rolls

INGREDIENTS

Dough

½ cup water

½ cup palm shortening

2 tablespoons maple syrup

½ teaspoon sea salt

1 cup tapioca flour

½ cup coconut flour

½ teaspoon ground cinnamon

1 large egg

Apple filling

2 tablespoons coconut oil

1 small Golden Delicious apple, peeled, cored, and diced

½ teaspoon sea salt

½ teaspoon ground cinnamon

¼ teaspoon ground nutmeg

Caramel frosting

1 cup canned, full-fat coconut milk

½ teaspoon vanilla extract

2 tablespoons maple syrup

NOTE: Before starting this recipe, check out the tips on working with tapioca flour (page 277).

1. Preheat the oven to 350°F. Line a rimmed baking sheet with parchment paper.

2. Make the dough: In a saucepan over medium heat, bring the water, palm shortening, maple syrup, and salt to a boil.

3. Add the tapioca flour, immediately remove from the heat, and stir with a fork to combine. Let cool for 2 to 3 minutes.

4. Add the coconut flour, cinnamon, and egg and mix until a soft dough forms.

5. Move the dough to a piece of parchment paper and knead it for 5 minutes.

6. Place a second piece of parchment paper on top of the dough and, with a rolling pin, roll the dough into a ½-inch-thick rectangle, roughly 7 inches by 9 inches. Set aside.

7. Make the filling: In a saucepan, cook the coconut oil and diced apple over medium heat for 8 minutes, or until the apple is soft. Add the salt, cinnamon, and nutmeg and mix with a spoon to coat the apple. Remove from the heat and spread the filling on top of the dough rectangle, leaving a ½-inch border on all sides.

8. Form and bake the rolls: With the short side facing you, roll the dough into a 7-inch-long log and trim the ends. Cut the log into six 1-inch pieces.

9. Place the rolls cut side down on the prepared baking sheet and bake for 28 to 30 minutes, until the dough is light golden brown and firm to the touch. Remove from the oven and let cool in the pan.

10. Make the frosting: In a saucepan over medium heat, combine the coconut milk, vanilla extract, and maple syrup. Bring to a boil and then decrease the heat to medium. Let simmer for 12 to 15 minutes, until it is reduced by half and is thick enough to coat a spoon. Drizzle the frosting over the top of the cinnamon rolls.

11. Store leftovers in the refrigerator for 3 to 4 days.

Cherry Toaster Pastries

One of my favorite memories from childhood is opening up my lunch box and finding these pastries inside. Now, many years later, I love to pack them in my son's lunch box as a surprise treat. Similar to the breakfast classic Pop-Tarts, these pastries are sure to leave sweet memories.

PREP TIME

20 min

COOK TIME
1 hour

MAKES
6 pastries

INGREDIENTS

Cherry filling

1½ cups fresh or frozen pitted cherries

¼ cup water

½ teaspoon vanilla extract

¼ teaspoon sea salt

2 tablespoons maple syrup

Dough

¼ cup water

¼ cup coconut oil

¼ cup maple syrup

1 teaspoon vanilla extract

¼ teaspoon sea salt

½ cup tapioca flour

½ cup unsweetened applesauce

½ cup coconut flour

Icing

1 teaspoon reserved cherry filling

¼ cup palm shortening

DIET

AIP

1. Preheat the oven to 350°F. Line a rimmed baking sheet with parchment paper or a silicone baking mat.

2. Make the filling: In a medium saucepan over medium heat, combine the cherries, water, vanilla extract, salt, and maple syrup and cook for 35 to 40 minutes, until reduced by half. Remove from the heat and set aside. Reserve 1 teaspoon for the icing.

3. Make the dough: In a medium saucepan, bring the water, coconut oil, maple syrup, vanilla extract, and salt to a boil. Remove from the heat. Add the tapioca flour and mix with a wooden spoon until well combined. Add the applesauce and coconut flour and mix until you have a soft dough.

4. Roll out the dough between two sheets of parchment paper until it is ¼ inch thick. Cut the dough into twelve 2-by-3-inch rectangles. Spoon 1 tablespoon of the cherry filling onto one rectangle, leaving a ¼-inch border. Cover with another rectangle and crimp the edges together to seal. Repeat with the rest of the rectangles and filling to make a total of six pastries.

5. Place the pastries on the prepared baking sheet and bake for 12 to 18 minutes, until light golden brown. Remove from the oven and cool completely on the pan.

6. Make the icing: In a small bowl, whisk the reserved teaspoon of cherry filling and the palm shortening together until completely smooth.

7. Frost the top of the cooled pastries.

8. Store the pastries in the fridge for 3 to 4 days. You can also freeze them. To reheat, remove them from the freezer and let them come to room temperature, then place them in a 275°F oven for 8 to 10 minutes.

Apple Fritters

Before I went Paleo, I was the queen of donuts. I'm pretty sure I ate five a week, and it's a miracle that I was able to walk away from them. This recipe helped: it's the perfect replacement for donuts and is scrumptious with coffee. You can make these fritters crispy, if you like more of a crunch, or soft, if you prefer a more donut-like texture.

PREP TIME 15 min

COOK TIME 20 min

MAKES 10 fritters

INGREDIENTS

½ cup coconut flour

½ cup tapioca flour

½ teaspoon sea salt

1 teaspoon pumpkin pie spice

2 large eggs

½ cup melted coconut oil

½ cup honey

¼ cup canned, full-fat coconut milk

1 medium Granny Smith apple, peeled, cored, and shredded

4 cups coconut oil, for frying

¼ cup Powdered Sugar (page 60)

1. In a large mixing bowl, combine the coconut flour, tapioca flour, salt, and pumpkin pie spice. Add the eggs, melted coconut oil, honey, and coconut milk and mix until smooth.

2. Place the shredded apple in a piece of cheesecloth and squeeze out the excess liquid. Mix the shredded apple into the batter until fully combined.

3. In a Dutch oven or large saucepan, heat the oil to 350°F.

4. With a large spoon, scoop up a portion of batter. Use a second large spoon to help drop the batter into the hot oil (see Note).

5. Repeat two or three times, being sure not to overcrowd the pan, and let the fritters cook until golden brown, roughly 3 minutes per side.

6. Remove the fritters from the oil and set on a paper towel to drain.

7. Sprinkle with the powdered sugar and serve immediately.

NOTE: For crispy fritters, press each scoop of batter between the two spoons to flatten it before dropping it in the hot oil. For soft, doughy fritters, drop a large scoop of batter in the hot oil without flattening it.

Pizza Crust

It took me years to find a Paleo pizza crust that my husband could stomach. He hated cauliflower crusts, loathed almond flour crusts, and despised Meatza (a crust primarily made of sausage and beef). But when he took his first bite of this crust, I'm pretty sure I saw happy little birdies flying around his head, and when he said, "Now that's a pizza crust," I knew I had hit the mark. Thin, crispy, and never soggy, this crust is a favorite in our home.

PREP TIME 15 min   COOK TIME 30 min   MAKES 1 (10-inch) crust

INGREDIENTS

½ cup water

⅓ cup extra-virgin olive oil or palm shortening

1 teaspoon sea salt

1 teaspoon garlic powder

½ teaspoon dried basil

1½ cups tapioca flour

1 large egg, beaten

2 tablespoons coconut flour

1. Preheat the oven to 350°F.

2. In a large saucepan over medium heat, bring the water, olive oil, salt, garlic powder, and basil to a boil. Add the tapioca flour and immediately remove from the heat.

3. Mix in the tapioca flour and keep stirring until you have a sticky dough.

4. Let the dough cool for 2 to 3 minutes and then place it in a medium mixing bowl. Add the egg and coconut flour. Mix and let sit for 1 minute to allow the coconut flour to thicken up. Once thickened, stir until it forms a uniform, soft dough that pulls away from the bowl.

5. Place the dough on a piece of parchment paper and knead until it forms a ball.

6. Place a second piece of parchment paper on top of the dough and roll it into a ¼-inch-thick, 10-inch circle.

7. Remove the top sheet of parchment and place the crust and bottom piece of parchment on a rimmed baking sheet.

8. Bake for 20 minutes, or until light golden brown. Remove from the oven and top with your favorite toppings. Return to the oven and bake for an additional 10 minutes.

NOTE: Before starting this recipe, check out the tips on working with tapioca flour (page 277).

Sweet Bread

This is my favorite recipe to make when I want a quick treat or am craving something to spread homemade Strawberry Jam (page 58) on. It's easy to make completely different breads just by adding a few ingredients to the main recipe. I've included two of my favorite variations below.

PREP TIME

10 min

COOK TIME

25 min

MAKES
1
(5-by-9-inch) loaf

INGREDIENTS

⅓ cup melted coconut oil, plus more for greasing the pan

5 large eggs, at room temperature

½ cup coconut flour

½ cup apple butter

½ teaspoon vanilla extract

½ teaspoon baking soda

1. Preheat the oven to 350°F. Grease a 5-by-9-inch loaf pan.

2. Place all of the ingredients in a blender and mix until thoroughly combined, roughly 1 minute.

3. Pour the batter into the prepared pan and bake for 20 to 25 minutes, until a toothpick inserted in the center comes out clean.

4. Remove from the oven and let cool in the pan for 15 minutes before slicing.

5. Store leftovers in an airtight container in the fridge for 2 to 3 days, or freeze and defrost as needed.

VARIATIONS

Chocolate Zucchini Bread

Grate 1 large zucchini. Place the grated zucchini in a nut milk bag or cheesecloth and squeeze to remove the excess water. After mixing up the main batter, add the zucchini and ¼ cup cacao powder to the blender. Mix with a spoon to incorporate and continue with step 3.

Banana Walnut Bread

Omit the apple butter. After mixing up the main batter, add 2 large ripe mashed bananas and ½ cup chopped raw walnuts to the blender. Mix with a spoon to incorporate and continue with step 3.

Yeasted Biscuits

The taste of these biscuits takes me back to the days when my mom made fresh bread that I ate hot out of the oven. I can do the same thing with these biscuits and not regret it a bit, because they're completely gluten-free. While the yeast gives these biscuits an amazing smell, taste, and texture, keep in mind that they won't fluff up and rise like biscuits made with gluten-based flour.

PREP TIME
30 min

COOK TIME
30 min

MAKES
24 biscuits

plus 2 hours to rise

INGREDIENTS

1 cup canned, full-fat coconut milk

1 cup water

½ cup melted palm shortening

1 tablespoon honey

1 (1¼-ounce) package active dry yeast

1 cup tapioca flour

½ cup coconut flour

5 cups blanched, superfine almond flour, divided

1 teaspoon sea salt

1. Warm the coconut milk, water, melted palm shortening, and honey in a saucepan. Remove from the heat and let cool to 115°F. Add the yeast and whisk. Let sit for 10 minutes.

2. Add the tapioca flour, coconut flour, 1 cup of the almond flour, and salt and mix until smooth. Let sit for 1 minute, then add an additional cup of the almond flour and mix. Repeat until the almond flour is gone, allowing the dough to rest for 1 minute after each addition of almond flour. The texture of the dough should be similar to a soft cookie dough. Cover and let sit in a warm place for 2 hours.

3. Preheat the oven to 350°F. Line two baking sheets with parchment paper.

4. Scoop a 2-inch piece of dough and shape it into a ball. Place the dough ball on a prepared baking sheet and press it to ½ inch thick. Repeat with the rest of the dough, placing the biscuits 2 inches apart on the baking sheets.

5. Place the biscuits in the oven and bake for 30 minutes, or until golden brown, switching the positions of the baking sheets halfway through. Remove from the oven and let cool on a cooling rack.

Grain-Free Wraps

Paleo breads can often taste too eggy. After fussing with this recipe, I finally got the egg count correct so that you taste only the wonderful flavor of the wraps, just as you remember from your pre-Paleo days. These wraps pair well with both savory and sweet foods, so they are very versatile.

PREP TIME

5
min

COOK TIME
40
min

MAKES
5
wraps

INGREDIENTS

3 large eggs

1 large egg white

¼ cup blanched, superfine almond flour

½ teaspoon sea salt

½ cup tapioca flour

¼ teaspoon baking soda

1 tablespoon coconut oil

1. Place the eggs, egg white, almond flour, salt, tapioca flour, and baking soda in a medium bowl. Whisk for 1 minute.

2. In a cast-iron skillet over medium heat, melt the coconut oil.

3. Pour a 5-inch circle of batter into the skillet. Cook for 3 to 4 minutes, until lightly browned in the center, and then flip and repeat on the other side.

4. Remove from the pan and repeat with the rest of the batter, whisking the ingredients before pouring each new wrap.

NOTE: It's possible to make wraps larger than 5 inches in diameter, but they're a little more challenging to work with. You'll need to push the wrap with a heat-resistant spatula to keep it a circle.

Sweet Potato Biscuits

These biscuits make me wish that I had the metabolism of teenage boy so I could wolf down a batch of these carbolicious gems and then cook up another to save for a snack. The sweet potatoes give them a buttery taste that will have you running to the kitchen to make more.

PREP TIME
15 min

plus 20 min for the mashed sweet potato

COOK TIME
20 min

MAKES
8 biscuits

INGREDIENTS

3 cups blanched, superfine almond flour

1 cup mashed sweet potato (1 small sweet potato; see Note)

¼ cup melted coconut oil

½ teaspoon baking soda

½ teaspoon sea salt

1 large egg, beaten

1. Preheat the oven to 350°F. Line a baking sheet with parchment paper or a silicone baking mat.

2. Combine all of the ingredients in a bowl and mix with a spoon until well blended. The dough will be sticky and wet.

3. You can scoop up a large spoonful of dough for drop biscuits, or wet your hands, pinch off a 2-inch piece of dough, and roll it into a ball.

4. Drop (or place, if using dough balls) the biscuits on the prepared baking sheet, spacing them 2 inches apart. If using dough balls, press to ½ inch thick.

5. Bake for 15 to 20 minutes, until lightly browned on top. Remove from the oven and let cool on a rack.

NOTE: To make approximately 1 cup of mashed sweet potato, peel 1 small sweet potato (about 12 ounces) and cut it into quarters. Place the pieces in a saucepan and cover with water (about 4 cups). Bring to a boil over high heat. Lower the heat to medium-high and cook for 15 to 18 minutes, until fork-tender. Drain well, return the sweet potatoes to the pan, and mash with a potato masher until smooth.

Basic Pie Crust

At first it might seem like this dough isn't going to come together properly, but trust me, it's amazingly sturdy and has a delicate taste at the same time. This is my go-to recipe for any dish, sweet or savory, that requires a pie crust. If you need both a top and a bottom crust, make sure you double the recipe.

PREP TIME	COOK TIME	MAKES
10 min	15 min	1 (8-inch) pie crust

INGREDIENTS

1¼ cups blanched, superfine almond flour

2 tablespoons coconut flour

¼ teaspoon sea salt

1 tablespoon melted coconut oil

1 large egg

1. Preheat the oven to 350°F.

2. Place the almond flour, coconut flour, and salt in a large bowl and mix with a fork.

3. Add the melted coconut oil and egg and blend with a wooden spoon until a dough forms.

4. Remove the dough from the bowl, place it on a piece of parchment paper, and knead for 30 seconds.

5. Place a second piece of parchment paper on top of the dough and, with a rolling pin, roll it into a ¼-inch-thick circle.

6. Remove the top piece of parchment, turn the dough into an 8-inch pie pan, and trim the edges. Pinch together any cracks or tears.

7. Bake for 15 minutes. Remove from the oven and let cool before filling.

Hamburger Buns

Sometimes you just need a hamburger bun to sop up the mess from a hamburger. These buns are sturdy and can handle a big load. I tend to go a bit overboard with Homemade Mayo (page 30), Ketchup (page 28), Honey Mustard (page 40), and onions, but these buns never fail me: they always keep everything together for every big, delicious bite. They're also great with Lamb Gyro Burgers (page 140).

PREP TIME	COOK TIME	MAKES
10 min	22 min	6 buns

INGREDIENTS

½ cup blanched, superfine almond flour

½ cup tapioca flour

¼ cup coconut flour

½ teaspoon baking powder

½ teaspoon baking soda

½ teaspoon sea salt

2 large eggs

½ cup water

½ teaspoon apple cider vinegar

1. Preheat the oven to 350°F. Grease a six-well hamburger bun pan (see Note).

2. In a large bowl, whisk together the almond flour, tapioca flour, coconut flour, baking powder, baking soda, and salt until thoroughly blended.

3. In a separate bowl, combine the eggs, water, and vinegar and mix until smooth.

4. Add the wet ingredients to the dry ingredients and blend completely until you have a thick batter.

5. Pour the batter into the wells of the greased hamburger bun pan and bake for 20 to 22 minutes, until light golden brown.

6. Remove the buns from the pan and let cool on a rack. Once cool, you can slice the buns in half.

NOTE: Don't have a hamburger bun pan? You can bake these buns on a baking sheet lined with parchment paper. Simply scoop up a burger bun–sized portion of batter and spread it into a 3-inch circle with a spatula.

Skillet Cornbread

This cornbread is light and sweet, and the texture reminds me of the classic cornbread I grew up eating. My father is from the South and loves cornbread, and this recipe even earned his nod of approval. It goes particularly well with Chili (page 142) and is delectable smothered in Strawberry Jam (page 58).

PREP TIME	COOK TIME	MAKES
10 min	40 min	8 servings

INGREDIENTS

¼ cup melted bacon fat or extra-virgin olive oil, plus more for greasing the pan (optional)

3 cups blanched, superfine almond flour

2 tablespoons coconut flour

½ teaspoon sea salt

½ teaspoon baking soda

½ teaspoon baking powder

2 tablespoons honey

2 large eggs

1¼ cups water

1. Preheat the oven to 350°F. If it's not yet seasoned, grease a 10-inch cast-iron skillet.

2. In a large mixing bowl, combine the almond flour, coconut flour, salt, baking soda, and baking powder and mix with a fork.

3. In a separate bowl, whisk together the melted bacon fat, honey, eggs, and water. Pour this mixture into the dry ingredients and mix with a spoon until you have a smooth batter.

4. Pour the batter into the prepared skillet and bake for 35 to 40 minutes, until a toothpick inserted in the center comes out clean.

5. Let sit for 10 minutes before serving.

Breadsticks

Why is it that food is so much more fun in stick form? I could not keep these breadsticks out of my son's hands, where they magically transformed from delicious treats into swords for a toddler. I couldn't help but smile as I watched him battle imaginary dragons and then take a huge bite after he won the fight. In addition to making great swords, these breadsticks are excellent with Chicken Parmesan (page 130).

PREP TIME
15 min

COOK TIME
18 min

MAKES
10–12 breadsticks

INGREDIENTS

1 cup blanched, superfine almond flour

½ cup tapioca flour

3 tablespoons coconut flour, divided

½ teaspoon dried oregano leaves

1 tablespoon melted coconut oil

2 large eggs

1. Preheat the oven to 350°F. Line a baking sheet with parchment paper or a silicone baking mat.

2. In a mixing bowl, whisk together the almond flour, tapioca flour, 2 tablespoons of the coconut flour, and oregano until thoroughly blended.

3. Mix in the melted coconut oil and eggs and blend until a sticky dough forms.

4. Spread the remaining 1 tablespoon of coconut flour on a piece of parchment paper and scoop the dough onto the floured surface. Knead the dough by hand until very smooth and soft, about 2 minutes.

5. Pinch off a 1-inch ball of dough and shape it into a 7-inch-long breadstick. Repeat with the remaining dough.

6. Place the breadsticks on the prepared baking sheet, 2 inches apart, and bake for 15 to 18 minutes, until golden brown.

7. Remove from the oven and let cool on a rack before serving.

Garlic Bread Rolls

If you've missed bread, these rolls are guaranteed to put a smile on your face. They're crispy on the outside and soft on the inside, similar to the French bread you remember. I like them with just about anything, but they go exceedingly well with Chicken Parmesan (page 130), Meatloaf (page 122), and Southern Fried Chicken (page 138). You can also freeze them and defrost as needed.

PREP TIME	COOK TIME	MAKES
15 min	30 min	5 rolls

INGREDIENTS

½ cup extra-virgin olive oil or palm shortening

½ cup water

1 teaspoon sea salt

½ teaspoon garlic powder

¾ cup tapioca flour

1 large egg

¼ cup coconut flour

1. Preheat the oven to 350°F. Line a baking sheet with parchment paper.

2. In a small saucepan, bring the olive oil, water, and salt to a boil. Remove from the heat and stir in the garlic powder and then the tapioca flour. Mix thoroughly with a fork and let rest for 5 minutes.

3. Stir in the egg and coconut flour and mix well until a soft dough forms.

4. Place the dough on the parchment paper and knead for 1 minute. Pinch off a 1-inch piece of dough, roll it into a ball, and place the ball on the prepared baking sheet. Repeat with the rest of the dough, spacing the balls 2 inches apart.

5. Bake for 25 to 30 minutes, until light golden brown.

6. Remove from the oven and let cool on a rack.

NOTE: Before starting this recipe, check out the tips on working with tapioca flour (page 277).

Raisin Bread

When I took my first bite of this bread, I was transported back to first grade and sharing a piece of raisin bread with my best friend. It was sweet and lightly nutty, and all I wanted to do was eat the entire piece. I figure any recipe that can bring back a memory like that has to be a winner, so I cut myself another slice and devoured it. When cold, this bread has a flavor similar to a Fig Newton.

PREP TIME

15 min

COOK TIME
40 min

MAKES
1
(5-by-9-inch)
loaf

INGREDIENTS

coconut oil, for greasing the pan

1 cup blanched, superfine almond flour

1 cup tapioca flour

2 tablespoons coconut flour

½ teaspoon baking soda

½ teaspoon baking powder

¼ teaspoon sea salt

1 teaspoon vanilla extract

2 large eggs

½ cup applesauce

2 tablespoons honey

1 teaspoon apple cider vinegar

1 cup raisins

1. Preheat the oven to 350°F. Grease a 5-by-9-inch loaf pan.

2. In a large mixing bowl, combine the almond flour, tapioca flour, coconut flour, baking soda, baking powder, and salt and blend well.

3. Add the vanilla extract, eggs, applesauce, honey, and vinegar and mix until you have a smooth, thick batter. Fold in the raisins.

4. Pour the batter into the prepared loaf pan. Bake for 35 to 40 minutes, until a toothpick inserted in the center comes out clean.

5. Let cool in the pan before slicing.

CHAPTER 3

BREAKFAST

Coconut Cinnamon Cereal

I grew up eating and loving Cinnamon Toast Crunch cereal, and I was determined to figure out how to create a grain-free version that would be perfect for a quick breakfast or snack. This is it! The key is unsweetened shredded coconut, which gives it a crispy crunch. I have a hard time keeping this cereal around—it disappears almost as soon as I make it.

PREP TIME

15 min

plus 15 min to cool

COOK TIME

15 min

MAKES
6 servings

INGREDIENTS

1 cup unsweetened shredded coconut

½ cup raw sunflower seeds

1 tablespoon ground cinnamon

¼ teaspoon sea salt

¼ cup maple syrup

1 large egg

½ teaspoon melted coconut oil

1. Preheat the oven to 350°F. Line a baking sheet with parchment paper.

2. Place the coconut and sunflower seeds in a food processor and grind for 30 seconds.

3. Add the cinnamon, salt, maple syrup, egg, and melted coconut oil and pulse until combined, about 2 minutes.

4. Scoop the mixture onto the prepared baking sheet. Cover with a second piece of parchment paper and, with a rolling pin, roll to ¼ inch thick. Remove and discard the top piece of parchment paper.

5. With a wet knife, score the dough into 1-inch squares.

6. Bake the cereal for 10 to 15 minutes, until firm to the touch. Remove from the oven and let sit on the baking sheet for 15 minutes to allow it to crisp up.

7. Store in an airtight jar in the refrigerator for up to a week.

Crustless Quiche

This killer recipe is one of the first that I Paleo-fied, so I could keep my mother-in-law happy—the saying "the way to a man's heart is through his stomach" also applies to mothers-in-law (and everyone else, truthfully). The combination of nutmeg and sage gives this quiche the power to win the heart of anyone you serve it to. For quick breakfasts, make it in a muffin pan and freeze the "breakfast cups."

PREP TIME
20 min

COOK TIME
35 min

MAKES
6 servings

INGREDIENTS

2 tablespoons coconut oil, plus more for greasing the pan

1 small yellow onion, diced

2 packed cups fresh spinach leaves, chopped

4 large eggs

1½ cups Coconut Milk (page 34)

1 tablespoon dried parsley leaves

½ teaspoon dried sage leaves

¼ teaspoon ground nutmeg

½ teaspoon sea salt

½ teaspoon ground black pepper

1. Preheat the oven to 350°F. Grease a 9-inch pie pan.

2. Melt the coconut oil in a skillet over medium heat. Add the onion and spinach and cook for 10 to 15 minutes, until the onions are slightly browned and the spinach is completely wilted. Place this mixture in the prepared pie pan and spread it evenly across the bottom. Set aside.

3. In a blender, blend the eggs, coconut milk, parsley, sage, nutmeg, salt, and pepper for 30 seconds, or until well mixed. Pour this mixture over the cooked vegetables.

4. Bake for 30 to 35 minutes, until a knife inserted about 1 inch from the edge comes out clean and the center jiggles loosely. Remove from the oven, cut into six wedges, and serve immediately.

Banana Pancakes

Flapjacks, hotcakes, griddle cakes—it doesn't matter what you call them, people will run to the kitchen for a bite of these fluffy pancakes. Ripe banana is the only sweetener, but you can always get creative and add chocolate chips or dates to make them extra fun. I love these pancakes with a touch of maple syrup and topped with fresh berries or cinnamon-coated diced apples. They also make a tasty portable snack when we're out and about during the day.

PREP TIME	COOK TIME	MAKES
5 min	8 min *per pancake*	7 (6-inch) pancakes

INGREDIENTS

1½ cups mashed ripe bananas (3 large bananas)

3 tablespoons coconut flour

3 large eggs

¾ teaspoon vanilla extract

¼ teaspoon sea salt

½ teaspoon baking soda

½ teaspoon ground cinnamon

3 tablespoons coconut oil, divided

1. Place the mashed bananas, coconut flour, eggs, vanilla extract, salt, baking soda, and cinnamon in a food processor or blender and mix until smooth, about 1 minute.

2. Heat a large cast-iron skillet over medium heat. Melt 1 tablespoon of the coconut oil.

3. Pour about ⅓ cup of batter into the skillet and cook until the underside of the pancake is light golden brown, roughly 3 to 4 minutes, and then flip and cook for another 3 to 4 minutes. Repeat with the rest of the batter, adding the remaining coconut oil as needed.

4. Serve immediately.

French Toast

French toast is a must for brunch—or really any occasion when you want to indulge. In this breakfast classic remake, thick slices of homemade Sweet Bread (page 74) are soaked in egg and coconut milk with a hint of cinnamon. You can eat it as-is or drizzle maple syrup or honey over the top for added sweetness. If you want to kick it up a notch, serve it topped with fresh berries or dusted with Powdered Sugar (page 60). Just remember to plan ahead so that you have a loaf of baked Sweet Bread on hand.

PREP TIME	COOK TIME	MAKES
10 min	8 min *per slice*	8 slices

INGREDIENTS

2 large eggs, beaten

½ cup canned, full-fat coconut milk

½ teaspoon vanilla extract

¼ teaspoon ground cinnamon

3 tablespoons coconut oil

1 loaf Sweet Bread (page 74), cut into ½-inch-thick slices

1. Place the eggs, coconut milk, vanilla extract, and cinnamon in a shallow pan or baking dish. With a spoon, mix until well blended.

2. Melt the coconut oil in a large skillet over medium heat.

3. Dip the bread slices in the coconut milk mixture and coat on both sides. Place in the skillet and cook until golden brown, about 4 minutes, and then flip and cook until browned on the other side. Repeat with the remaining bread slices and batter. Serve immediately.

Mock Oatmeal

Nothing says "good morning" like a bowl of steaming hot oatmeal. When winter hits us in Portland and the rain just won't end, I like to curl up with a bowl of this nut-and-seed-based mock oatmeal and a book. The dates add a rich, buttery sweetness that can't be beat. Be sure not to overprocess the oatmeal starter, as the rough texture of the nuts helps re-create the oatmeal feel.

PREP TIME   COOK TIME   MAKES

10 min   5 min   1 serving

INGREDIENTS

1 cup raw hazelnuts

¼ cup raw sunflower seeds

¼ cup chia seeds

15 whole Deglet Noor dates, pitted

½ teaspoon ground cinnamon

½ teaspoon sea salt

½ cup Coconut Milk (page 34)

½ cup pitted cherries or other fruit, for topping (optional)

1. Place all of the ingredients except the coconut milk and cherries in a food processor and pulse until you have a rough crumble. Set aside ½ cup of this starter to use immediately and store the remainder in an airtight container for up to 1 month. This recipe makes enough starter for 3 servings of oatmeal.

2. In a saucepan, combine the reserved ½ cup of the oatmeal starter and the coconut milk and place over medium heat. Stir and bring to a boil, then lower the heat and cook for 2 to 3 minutes, until thick and creamy.

3. Remove from the heat and top with cherries or your favorite fruit, if desired. Serve immediately.

Breakfast Burrito

Having spent a large portion of my life in Arizona, I know my way around a burrito. Breakfast burritos are not meant to be fancy—they are a quick way to get in a delicious meal. How can you resist fluffy eggs, cilantro, and salsa verde all wrapped up in a delicious tortilla? I love mine piled high with caramelized onions and black olives.

PREP TIME	COOK TIME	MAKES
10 min	10 min	2 servings

INGREDIENTS

2 Grain-Free Wraps (page 78)

Filling

2 tablespoons coconut oil

½ small yellow onion, diced

3 large eggs

¼ teaspoon sea salt

¼ teaspoon ground black pepper

2 tablespoons chopped fresh cilantro

2 tablespoons Salsa Verde (page 56)

Optional toppings

cooked Breakfast Sausage (page 108)

cooked diced bacon

sliced black olives

caramelized onions

1. If you don't have any wraps on hand, make them and set them aside.

2. Make the filling: Melt the coconut oil in a skillet over medium heat. Add the onion and sauté until lightly browned, about 5 to 7 minutes.

3. In a small bowl, whisk the eggs with the salt and pepper.

4. Pour the beaten eggs into the skillet and add the cilantro. Using a heat-resistant rubber spatula, move the eggs around in the skillet until cooked to your liking.

5. Remove the eggs from the heat. Divide them between two wraps and top with the salsa verde and additional toppings of your choice, if desired, being careful not to overfill the wraps.

6. Fold the bottom of the wrap a quarter of the way up and over the eggs, then fold over the left and right sides of the wrap, and continue rolling to enclose the filling and toppings.

Breakfast Sausage

I had no idea how easy it was to make breakfast sausage until I began working on this recipe. The sage, thyme, marjoram, and allspice blend together to create an amazing flavor. If you want to spice it up, try adding red pepper flakes or cayenne to the mix.

PREP TIME
10 min

COOK TIME
15 min

MAKES
4 patties

INGREDIENTS

2 teaspoons dried sage leaves

½ teaspoon dried thyme leaves

¼ teaspoon dried marjoram leaves

⅛ teaspoon ground allspice

1 teaspoon sea salt

1 teaspoon ground black pepper

1 pound ground pork

1. Combine the sage, thyme, marjoram, allspice, salt, and pepper in a small bowl and mix well with a spoon.

2. In a medium bowl, combine the ground pork and spice blend and mix well with a fork.

3. With your hands, shape the meat into four ½-inch-thick patties about 3 inches in diameter.

4. In a large skillet over medium-high heat, cook the patties for 5 to 7 minutes, until browned. Flip and cook for another 5 to 7 minutes. Serve immediately.

Granola

This recipe is wickedly delicious. I try not to make it too often because it evaporates into thin air—that is, into my stomach—at an incredible speed. The combination of dates and black pepper creates a sweet and spicy flavor that is just luscious. This granola is fantastic as a cereal, snack, or ice cream topping.

PREP TIME
20 min

plus 3 hours to cool

COOK TIME
15 min

MAKES
4 cups

INGREDIENTS

coconut oil, for greasing the pan

15 whole Deglet Noor dates, pitted

¼ teaspoon ground black pepper

1 tablespoon fresh lemon juice

¼ teaspoon ground allspice

¼ teaspoon sea salt

1 large egg white

1 cup raw pecans

1 cup unsweetened coconut flakes

1 cup raw slivered almonds

1 cup raw pumpkin seeds

1. Preheat the oven to 350°F. Grease a rimmed baking sheet.

2. Place the dates, pepper, lemon juice, allspice, and salt in a food processor and pulse for 30 seconds.

3. Add the egg white and pulse for 10 seconds to combine.

4. In a large bowl, combine the pecans, coconut flakes, slivered almonds, and pumpkin seeds and mix with a spoon.

5. With a nonstick spatula, scoop the date mixture into the bowl with the nuts and coconut and blend until fully coated.

6. Scoop the mixture onto the prepared baking sheet. Bake for 12 to 15 minutes, until fragrant and light golden brown.

7. Remove the granola from the oven and let cool on the pan for at least 3 hours. Store in an airtight container in the refrigerator for up to 2 weeks.

Over-Easy Eggs Benedict

Eggs Benedict is traditionally made with poached eggs, but I have a hard time focusing on getting poached eggs perfect with my toddler running in circles around me. I've found that over-easy eggs work just as well. If you prefer poached eggs, though, then go for it! Instructions are in the variation, below.

PREP TIME	COOK TIME	MAKES
15 min	2 min	2 servings

INGREDIENTS

Blender hollandaise sauce

3 large pastured egg yolks

1 tablespoon plus 1 teaspoon lemon juice

1 teaspoon apple cider vinegar

½ teaspoon sea salt

½ cup walnut oil

1 tablespoon coconut oil

4 large eggs

4 slices Black Forest ham

2 Sweet Potato Biscuits (page 80)

½ cup spinach leaves

1. Make the hollandaise sauce: Place the egg yolks, lemon juice, vinegar, and salt in a blender. Blend on medium speed for 15 to 20 seconds, until it lightens in color.

2. Reduce the speed to the lowest setting and slowly drizzle in the walnut oil until you have a smooth sauce. Set aside.

3. Melt the coconut oil in a large skillet over medium-low heat. As soon as the coconut oil has melted, crack the eggs in the pan. Cook for 30 seconds, or until the egg whites start to firm up. With a spatula, carefully flip the eggs and cook for another 30 seconds. Transfer to a plate.

4. Decrease the heat to low and place the ham in the skillet to warm it.

5. Slice the biscuits in half and top each half with a slice of ham, a few spinach leaves, and an egg. Pour the hollandaise sauce over the top and serve immediately.

VARIATION: EGGS BENEDICT WITH POACHED EGGS

To make poached eggs, bring 4 cups of water just to the point of boiling in a deep sauté pan or skillet. Reduce the heat to medium and add 1 teaspoon of apple cider vinegar. Using tongs, lower 4 small-mouth metal mason jar rings into the water. Working with one egg at a time, crack an egg into a small heatproof cup. Place the cup just above the surface of the hot water and slowly slide the egg into the center of a mason jar ring. This will help keep the egg whites from spreading out. Repeat with 3 more eggs. Turn off the heat and poach until the egg whites are cooked, approximately 4 minutes. Remove the eggs with a slotted spoon.

Berry Parfait

Fresh ripe berries, panna cotta, and homemade granola combine to create the perfect grab-and-go treat for breakfast. My husband and son tear through this parfait like a tornado though a trailer park. It runs on the sweeter side, so you can omit the maple syrup if you find it too sweet.

PREP TIME

10 min

COOK TIME

10 min

MAKES
2 servings

plus 2 hours to chill

INGREDIENTS

Panna cotta

1 (13½-ounce) can full-fat coconut milk

1 teaspoon vanilla extract

1 tablespoon maple syrup

½ teaspoon sea salt

1 tablespoon beef gelatin

1 large egg yolk, at room temperature

1 cup Granola (page 110)

1 cup fresh berries of choice (if using strawberries, hull and halve or quarter them)

1. Make the panna cotta: In a saucepan over medium heat, bring the coconut milk, vanilla extract, maple syrup, and salt to a boil.

2. Remove from the heat and set aside. Let cool for 3 to 5 minutes.

3. Meanwhile, in a small heatproof bowl, combine the gelatin and egg yolk.

4. Slowly whisk ¼ cup of the coconut milk mixture into the gelatin and egg mixture, then pour the gelatin and egg yolk mixture back into the saucepan and whisk for 30 seconds.

5. Pour into a glass container and chill, covered, for 2 hours.

6. Assemble the parfaits: In two small glasses, layer ¼ cup of the panna cotta, then ¼ cup of the granola, followed by fresh berries. Repeat for two layers of each.

Broccolini and Sweet Potato Omelet

When I'm not getting enough vegetables in my diet, this is the dish I turn to. There is something special about the tartness of lemon combined with the sweetness of sweet potato and bitter broccolini—all piled into a savory omelet. I liken this joyride of flavors to a savory breakfast pizza, but I also often whip it up for dinner.

PREP TIME	COOK TIME	MAKES
20 min	15 min	4 servings

plus 20 min for the mashed sweet potato

INGREDIENTS

Broccolini layer

1 tablespoon coconut oil

1 clove garlic, chopped

½ small yellow onion, diced (1 cup)

1½ cups diced broccolini

1 teaspoon lemon juice

¼ teaspoon sea salt

¼ teaspoon ground black pepper

Sweet potato layer

½ cup mashed sweet potato (½ small sweet potato; see Note, page 80)

¼ cup Coconut Milk (page 34)

⅛ teaspoon ground cinnamon

⅛ teaspoon dried crushed rosemary

¼ teaspoon sea salt

¼ teaspoon ground black pepper

Omelet

1 tablespoon coconut oil

3 large eggs

¼ teaspoon sea salt

¼ teaspoon ground black pepper

1. Make the broccolini layer: In a small skillet, combine the coconut oil, garlic, and onion and sauté until the onion is translucent, roughly 5 minutes. Add the broccolini, lemon juice, salt, and pepper and cook until lightly browned, about 4 minutes. Set aside on a warmer.

2. Make the sweet potato layer: Bring all of the ingredients for the layer to a boil in a small saucepan. Set aside on a warmer.

3. Make the omelet: Heat the coconut oil in a large skillet over medium-low heat.

4. In a large bowl, whisk the eggs with the salt and pepper. Pour the beaten eggs into the hot oil. Let the eggs cook undisturbed for 1 minute, until the bottom starts to firm up. Tilt the pan and let the liquid eggs run under the edge of the omelet and cook until the eggs are set and there is no more runny liquid left.

5. Gently flip the omelet and cook for a couple of seconds until there is no uncooked egg left.

6. Place the omelet on a plate and then cover with the sweet potato layer followed by the broccolini layer. Cut into four wedges and serve immediately.

CHAPTER 4

MAINS

Oven-Baked Dry-Rubbed Ribs

Who says you need a grill to enjoy ribs? These oven-baked ribs come out tender and perfectly seasoned. They're great on their own, but if you want, you can slather on some homemade Barbecue Sauce (page 26) and eat them with Sweet Potato Salad (page 196) or a green salad.

PREP TIME   COOK TIME   MAKES

15
min

3
hours

4
servings

INGREDIENTS

Rub

2 tablespoons cacao powder

1 tablespoon ground cumin

1 teaspoon dry mustard

2 teaspoons sea salt

½ teaspoon ground black pepper

2 racks baby back ribs, roughly 2 pounds each

OCCASION

Game day

1. Preheat the oven to 350°F.

2. In a small bowl, combine the ingredients for the rub and mix with a spoon.

3. Coat both sides of the racks of ribs with the spice rub.

4. Tear off four pieces of foil slightly longer than the ribs. Place one piece shiny side down and set a rack on it. Place the second piece of foil on top, dull side down, and pinch the corners and sides shut, creating a sealed packet. Repeat with the second rack and remaining pieces of foil.

5. Place the rib packets on a rimmed baking sheet and bake for 3 hours, until the ribs are blackened and the meat is falling off the bone.

Meatloaf

We always have baked sweet potatoes in the fridge, so I thought it would be fun to add them to meatloaf and see what happened. Thankfully, it was amazing! I will never forget the day I made this meatloaf for my father-in-law and he plowed through it bite after bite, murmuring how it was wonderful as he helped himself to seconds. He did point out, however, that it would be better with ketchup on top. He was right: don't forget to add the homemade ketchup.

PREP TIME COOK TIME MAKES

15 min

1 hour

6 servings

plus 20 min for the mashed sweet potato

INGREDIENTS

1 small yellow onion, peeled

2 pounds ground beef (85% lean)

1 cup mashed sweet potato, packed (1 small sweet potato; see Note, page 80)

2 tablespoons coconut flour

2 teaspoons sea salt

1½ teaspoons dried cilantro leaves

1½ teaspoons garlic powder

½ teaspoon ground black pepper

¼ teaspoon cayenne pepper

¾ cup Ketchup (page 28), for serving

1. Preheat the oven to 350°F.

2. Place the onion in a food processor and mince it.

3. In a large bowl, combine the minced onion and the remaining ingredients, except the ketchup. Mix with a spoon until well blended.

4. Transfer the meat mixture to a 4-by-8-inch loaf pan and shape into a loaf, smoothing out the top.

5. Bake for 1 hour.

6. Remove from the oven and top with the ketchup.

Chicken Katsu

Even the pickiest of kids (and adults) will love this dish. The breading is incredible, and you can easily make it into chicken fingers by slicing the chicken breasts into 1-inch-wide strips before breading and frying. This chicken goes well with Teriyaki Sauce (page 36) or Thai Almond Sauce (page 52) and steamed broccoli.

PREP TIME
15 min

COOK TIME
16 min

MAKES
4 servings

INGREDIENTS

1 cup lard or coconut oil

1 cup blanched, superfine almond flour

1 tablespoon tapioca flour

1 tablespoon coconut flour

½ teaspoon garlic powder

1 large egg

2 tablespoons water

2 boneless, skinless chicken breasts (1 pound), cut in half crosswise and pounded to ½ inch thick

½ teaspoon sea salt

1 teaspoon ground black pepper

1. Heat the lard in a skillet over medium heat.

2. In a paper bag, combine the almond flour, tapioca flour, coconut flour, and garlic powder. Close the bag and shake to combine.

3. In a small bowl, mix the egg and water and set aside.

4. Season the chicken pieces with the salt and pepper, dip into the egg wash, and place in the bag with the flour mixture. Shake the bag to evenly to coat the chicken.

5. Lower the coated chicken into the hot oil and cook until golden brown, about 5 to 8 minutes. Flip and cook for 5 to 8 minutes on the other side. Drain on a paper towel.

6. Serve immediately.

Pancit

When I was growing up, we ate this noodle-based dish at every celebration—birthdays, weddings, Thanksgiving, even St. Patrick's Day—always accompanied by sweet potato salad. I've adapted my mother's recipe here, and I knew I had hit the mark when I wanted to make a batch of sweet potato salad to go with it. Yes, this is a flashback from my past, a carb fest made in heaven.

PREP TIME	COOK TIME	MAKES
15 min	20 min	6 servings

INGREDIENTS

1 medium sweet potato, peeled

6 cups water

1 tablespoon extra-virgin olive oil

1 small yellow onion, diced (about 1½ cups)

2 cloves garlic, minced

1 pound boneless, skinless chicken breast, diced

½ cup Chicken Bone Broth (page 44)

2 tablespoons coconut aminos

1 teaspoon sea salt

¼ teaspoon ground black pepper

1 stalk celery, diced (⅓ cup)

½ head cabbage, cut into 1-by-3-inch strips (3 cups)

1 large carrot, peeled and cut into matchsticks

DIET

AIP

1. Using the small noodle setting on a spiral slicer, cut the sweet potato into noodles.

2. Bring the water to a boil in large saucepan and add the sweet potato noodles. Cook for 3 to 5 minutes. Drain and set aside.

3. In a large skillet over medium heat, combine the olive oil, onion, and garlic. Cook until the onion is translucent, about 3 minutes. Add the diced chicken, broth, coconut aminos, salt, and pepper and cook until the chicken is cooked through, about 10 minutes.

4. Add the celery, cabbage, carrot, and drained noodles to the skillet. With two large forks, lightly toss the ingredients to coat with the sauce. Serve immediately.

Sloppy Joes

Get ready to get messy when you bite into this dish. Quick, easy, and inexpensive, sloppy joes are a staple in a busy mom's meal plan. The blackstrap molasses gives it a nice, rich finish—don't be surprised if you don't have leftovers.

PREP TIME   COOK TIME   MAKES

 10 min   20 min   4 servings

INGREDIENTS

1 tablespoon extra-virgin olive oil

1 small yellow onion, diced

1 pound ground beef (85% lean)

2 teaspoons garlic powder

1½ teaspoons sea salt

½ teaspoon ground black pepper

2 tablespoons tomato paste

1 tablespoon blackstrap molasses

4 to 5 leaves romaine or butter leaf lettuce

1 batch Creamy Cucumber Dill Salad (page 176), for serving

Hot Sauce (page 46), for serving (optional)

1. In a skillet over medium heat, combine the olive oil and diced onion. Sauté until the onion is translucent, roughly 3 to 4 minutes.

2. Add the ground beef, garlic powder, salt, pepper, tomato paste, and molasses and mix with a spoon until well combined.

3. Cook for 10 to 15 minutes, until the beef is well-done.

4. Remove the beef mixture from the heat and place ½ cup in a lettuce leaf. Top with the cucumber salad and hot sauce, if desired. Repeat three times, for four servings total, and serve.

Chicken Parmesan

Crispy chicken smothered in flavorful spaghetti sauce will have everyone asking for seconds. Trust me, you won't miss the cheese that's in traditional chicken parmesan, and the pork rinds add a crunch your whole family will love. This is my son's favorite dinner, and it's amazing over Zucchini Noodles (page 210) and served with Breadsticks (page 88).

PREP TIME   COOK TIME   MAKES

 15 min   30 min   4 servings

INGREDIENTS

1 cup coconut oil, plus more for greasing the pan

1 (3½-ounce) bag pork rinds

½ cup coconut flour

½ teaspoon sea salt

½ teaspoon ground black pepper

2 large eggs

4 boneless, skinless chicken breasts (2 pounds), cut in half crosswise

1 cup Slow Cooker Spaghetti Sauce (page 50)

1. Preheat the oven to 375°F. Grease a 9-by-13-inch baking dish.

2. Place the pork rinds in a food processor and pulse until you have fine crumbs. Transfer to a paper bag.

3. Combine the coconut flour, salt, and pepper in a separate paper bag.

4. Crack the eggs into a large bowl and whisk.

5. Place the chicken breasts in the bag with the coconut flour mixture and shake to evenly coat the chicken. Remove the chicken breasts from the bag and dip in the beaten eggs, then drop them into the bag with the ground pork rinds, shaking the bag to thoroughly coat the chicken. Remove the chicken from the bag and set aside.

6. In a large skillet over medium heat, heat the coconut oil to 350°F.

7. Cook the chicken in the skillet until golden brown, roughly 3 to 5 minutes per side. Flip and repeat.

8. Place the chicken in the prepared baking dish and top with the spaghetti sauce.

9. Bake for 20 minutes. Remove from the oven and serve immediately.

Salmon Cakes

Before I moved to Oregon, I had no idea what salmon was or how to pronounce it properly (turns out the "L" is silent). Anyhow, my first taste of salmon was like "whoa," and not in a good way. I soon discovered that simply removing the skin makes the flavor much milder and more delicious, which is why I recommend using skinless canned salmon here. The flavorful melody of the salmon and the mixture of onions, celery, and dill will make this your favorite quick and easy dish.

PREP TIME
15 min

COOK TIME
12 min

MAKES
4 patties

INGREDIENTS

1 (6-ounce) can boneless, skinless salmon, drained

½ medium yellow onion, minced

1 stalk celery, diced

1 tablespoon dried dill weed

1 teaspoon lemon pepper

¼ teaspoon sea salt

1 tablespoon plus 1 teaspoon coconut flour

2 large eggs, beaten

1 tablespoon coconut oil

lemon wedges, for serving

1. Place the drained salmon in a bowl and use a fork to break it into pieces.

2. Mix in the onion, celery, dill, lemon pepper, salt, and coconut flour and blend thoroughly with a fork. Add the eggs and mix for 30 seconds.

3. Melt the coconut oil in a skillet over medium-high heat.

4. Shape the salmon mixture into four patties roughly 2 inches in diameter.

5. Add the patties to the skillet and cook until golden brown, roughly 4 to 6 minutes on each side.

6. Serve with lemon wedges.

NOTE: To quickly mince an onion, place it in a food processor and pulse for 30 seconds.

Ginger Chicken

This is, hands-down, my favorite recipe from childhood, and it was a happy surprise when I realized that it's Paleo-friendly. I proudly admit that I hoard the ginger sauce from this recipe because it is absolutely divine.

PREP TIME

 15 min

COOK TIME

 40 min

MAKES

4 servings

INGREDIENTS

1 tablespoon coconut oil

1 small yellow onion, chopped

1 (2½-inch) piece fresh ginger, peeled and sliced

2 pounds chicken legs

1 teaspoon sea salt

½ teaspoon ground black pepper

2 tablespoons diced red onion

DIET

 AIP

1. Combine the coconut oil, onion, and ginger in a skillet over medium heat and cook for 3 minutes, or until the onion is translucent.

2. Place the chicken legs in the skillet and season with the salt and pepper. Cover with a lid.

3. Reduce the heat to low and cook, covered, for 35 to 40 minutes. The chicken legs will release juices, creating a gingery sauce. Add the red onion during the last 3 minutes of cooking.

4. Optional: For more color on the chicken, remove the cooked legs from the skillet and broil for 3 to 5 minutes before serving.

Pepper Steak

I ate this dish every Thursday growing up. I began to think of it as Thursday pepper steak, and the savory gravy of onions, tomatoes, spices, and beef had me counting down the days until I could have it again. Every so often, I make pepper steak on Thursday just for the memories—and to keep my belly happy. This dish pairs well with Garlic Fried Rice (page 180).

PREP TIME
15 min

COOK TIME
18 min

MAKES
4 servings

INGREDIENTS

1 tablespoon coconut oil

½ small yellow onion, diced

3 cloves garlic, minced

1 (½-inch) piece ginger, peeled and chopped

1 Roma tomato, diced

1 pound sirloin steak, cut crosswise into thin strips

¼ teaspoon sea salt

¼ teaspoon ground black pepper

1 medium red bell pepper, seeded and sliced into thin strips

1. In a skillet over medium-high heat, melt the coconut oil. Add the onion, garlic, ginger, and tomato and cook for 3 minutes, or until the onion is translucent.

2. Add the steak, salt, and pepper and mix until well coated.

3. Cover with a lid. Reduce the heat to medium-low and cook for 10 minutes.

4. Add the bell pepper, cover, and cook for 5 minutes.

5. Remove from the heat and serve immediately.

Southern Fried Chicken

I regret not writing down my father-in-law's recipe for fried chicken before he passed away, but this version, patched together from his family's memories and with my own grain-free spin, comes close. Marinating the chicken in the tomatoes and spices makes it really juicy and punches up the flavor. This dish pairs well with Mashed "Potatoes" (page 178), Sweet Potato Salad (page 196), Creamy Cucumber Dill Salad (page 176), and Honey Ginger Carrots (page 186).

PREP TIME COOK TIME MAKES

15 min

40 min

6 servings

plus 4 hours to marinate

INGREDIENTS

Marinade

1 (14½-ounce) can diced tomatoes, no added salt

1 tablespoon sea salt

½ teaspoon ground black pepper

½ teaspoon garlic powder

½ teaspoon dried oregano leaves

1 teaspoon dried parsley leaves

2 pounds bone-in chicken pieces

4 cups bacon fat, coconut oil, or lard

Coating

1½ cups tapioca flour

1 teaspoon sea salt

1 teaspoon ground black pepper

1. In a large bowl, combine the ingredients for the marinade. Add the chicken pieces to the bowl and toss to evenly coat with the marinade. Cover and place in the refrigerator for 3 to 4 hours.

2. Remove the chicken from the refrigerator and let sit at room temperature for 10 to 15 minutes.

3. In a large cast-iron skillet over medium-high heat, heat the bacon fat to 325°F. Try to keep the oil no hotter than 325°F.

4. Make the coating: Place the tapioca flour, salt, and pepper in a large paper bag and shake to combine. Drop the chicken pieces into the bag and shake to coat on all sides.

5. Place the chicken in the hot oil and cook until golden brown on both sides, roughly 10 to 15 minutes per side, being careful not to overcrowd the pan. The internal temperature should reach 160°F. Remove the chicken from the pan and set on a rack over a rimmed baking sheet to cool.

6. Repeat step 5 until all of the chicken pieces have been fried. *Note:* If the chicken is golden brown on the outside but not yet fully cooked on the inside, set it on a rack over a rimmed baking sheet and place in a 350°F oven to finish cooking, roughly 8 to 10 minutes.

TIPS FOR PERFECT FRIED CHICKEN

1. For even heat and browning, cooking in cast iron is key.

2. Don't crowd the pan. For the chicken to cook properly, it needs to be surrounded by hot oil. Overcrowding the pan also causes the temperature of the oil to drop, resulting in greasy, soggy food.

3. Frying in bacon fat takes this recipe from "Wow, this is good" to "I want to marry this chicken!"

4. Try to keep the chicken pieces roughly the same size so they cook in the same amount of time. A simple way to do this is to cook legs together, thighs together, and so on.

5. To reheat this chicken, place it in a 350°F oven for 15 to 20 minutes. It will be crispy and finger-licking good.

TIPS FOR DEEP-FRYING

1. Use a saturated fat such as coconut oil, lard, or tallow, as it is less prone to oxidation and has a high smoke point.

2. Don't crowd the pan (see note on previous page).

3. You can reuse your cooking oil by allowing it to cool and, while it's still in liquid form, straining it though cheesecloth. Store it in a sealable container in a cool, dark place. When the oil darkens or starts to smell off or sour, discard it. I typically use oil four or five times before discarding.

Lamb Gyro Burgers

The first time I tried a gyro, I was hooked. The amazing combination of spices makes for a lip-smacking, unforgettable dish, and I had to try my hand at using gyro spices in this recipe. This gyro burger is perfectly seasoned and moist, and with patties instead of lamb slices and hamburger buns instead of pitas, it's much less work than a traditional gyro. Truth be told, I could eat these for a whole month and not get bored with them. I love them topped with Tahini Sauce (page 42), put on Hamburger Buns (page 84), and served with Creamy Caesar Salad (page 198) or Creamy Cucumber Dill Salad (page 176).

PREP TIME **20** min COOK TIME **10** min MAKES **4** patties

INGREDIENTS

1 tablespoon dried parsley

½ teaspoon dried oregano

½ teaspoon ground cumin

½ teaspoon dried crushed rosemary

½ teaspoon dried thyme

½ teaspoon ground black pepper

½ teaspoon ground coriander

¼ teaspoon ground cinnamon

1 teaspoon sea salt

½ medium yellow onion, peeled

5 cloves garlic, peeled

1 pound ground lamb

1 tablespoon extra-virgin olive oil

1 tablespoon coconut oil

1. In a small bowl, combine the spices and salt and mix with a spoon until well blended.

2. In a food processor, pulse the onion and garlic for 20 seconds, or until completely chopped.

3. Add the ground lamb to the food processor. Sprinkle the spice blend evenly over the lamb, then pour in the olive oil.

4. Pulse for 30 seconds to combine. Do not overprocess the meat, as it will change the texture. If the spices and meat are not fully combined after 30 seconds, use a spoon to blend the spices into the meat.

5. Form the meat into four 4-inch patties, about 1 inch thick, and set aside.

6. Melt the coconut oil in a large skillet over medium-high heat.

7. Add the patties to the skillet and cook until golden brown on both sides, roughly 4 to 5 minutes per side.

8. Remove from the heat and serve immediately.

Chili

Chili is not chili to me unless it tastes like the canned variety that I guzzled with abandon in my youth. This recipe is similar but even better—the flavors from the broth and fish sauce make it so much richer. I love digging into this chili with a big piece of Skillet Cornbread (page 86).

PREP TIME
15 min

COOK TIME
35 min

MAKES
2 servings

INGREDIENTS

2 tablespoons bacon fat or coconut oil

1 large yellow onion, diced

1 medium red bell pepper, seeded and diced

⅓ pound ground beef (85% lean)

1¼ teaspoons sea salt

3 tablespoons chili powder

1 teaspoon ground black pepper

1 teaspoon dried oregano leaves

1 teaspoon garlic powder

¼ teaspoon dried thyme leaves

1 tablespoon cacao powder

1 (14½-ounce) can diced tomatoes, no added salt

2 tablespoons tomato paste

½ teaspoon fish sauce

1 cup Chicken Bone Broth (page 44)

sliced green onion, for garnish (optional)

1. In a large pot over medium-high heat, melt the bacon fat. Add the onion and bell pepper and cook until the onion is lightly browned, roughly 5 minutes.

2. Add the ground beef, salt, spices, and cacao powder and mix with a spoon. Cook for 2 minutes.

3. Add the diced tomatoes, tomato paste, fish sauce, and broth. Mix with a spoon, reduce the heat to medium-low, and cook, covered, for 30 minutes.

4. Ladle into two serving bowls and garnish with the green onion, if desired.

Pho Ga

Until recently, I called this dish "Whey Soup" after my childhood neighbor who often brought over huge pots of it for us to eat. It wasn't until my husband took me out for pho that I realized that they are one and the same. This recipe is so simple, yet it's fragrant with spices. It's also rich with gelatin, which you will see when you remove this broth from the fridge. Don't skip charring the onion and ginger: it really brings the flavors together.

PREP TIME COOK TIME MAKES
20 min · 3¼ hours · 6 servings

INGREDIENTS

1 (3-inch) piece ginger (do not peel)

1 large yellow onion, halved

4½ pounds bone-in, skin-on chicken thighs

12 cups water

6 cloves garlic, roughly chopped

4 whole cloves

3 star anise

2 (3-inch) sticks cinnamon

3 tablespoons coconut aminos

1 tablespoon honey

2 teaspoons sea salt

Optional add-ins

bean spouts

sliced red onion

sliced green onion

cooked broccoli florets

cooked carrot slices

cooked Zucchini Noodles (page 210)

fresh cilantro

fresh Thai basil

1. Preheat the broiler to high. Set an oven rack in the top position.

2. Place the ginger and onion halves cut side up on a rimmed baking sheet. Broil for 15 minutes, turning the pieces halfway through to get an even char.

3. Remove the ginger and onion from the oven and let cool. Slice the charred ginger into several pieces.

4. Place the ginger pieces and onion in a large stockpot along with the chicken thighs and water. Add the garlic, cloves, star anise, and cinnamon.

5. Bring to a boil, then lower the heat to medium and let simmer for 3 hours, covered. After 1 hour, use a slotted spoon to remove the scum that has risen to the top.

6. When the broth has been simmering for 2½ hours, add the coconut aminos, honey, and salt and mix well.

7. After 3 hours, remove the pot from the heat and strain the broth through a strainer lined with cheesecloth.

8. Pick the meat off the chicken thighs and put it in a separate container.

9. To serve, place ½ cup of the chicken meat and the add-ins of your choice, if desired, in a soup bowl. Pour 3 cups of hot broth over the top and serve immediately.

10. Store leftover broth in an airtight jar in the refrigerator for up to a week. The chicken meat will last for 3 to 4 days in the fridge.

Kung Pao Chicken

This Szechuan dish is a favorite in our household. This recipe is a little less spicy than normal, because I take the heat down for my son, but you can easily add red pepper flakes to bring it back up. The roasted almonds give it a nice crunch, and the savory sauce is to die for. You may want to make double the sauce since it disappears so quickly. This dish is wonderful with Garlic Fried Rice (page 180) and steamed broccoli.

PREP TIME
10 min

COOK TIME
15 min

MAKES
4
servings

plus 30 min to marinate

INGREDIENTS

Marinade

1 tablespoon apple cider vinegar

1 tablespoon coconut aminos

1 tablespoon toasted sesame oil

1 tablespoon tapioca flour

1 pound boneless, skinless chicken breasts, cut into 1-inch cubes

Sauce

3 tablespoons coconut aminos

1 tablespoon apple cider vinegar

1 tablespoon toasted sesame oil

1 tablespoon tapioca flour

2 tablespoons Hot Sauce (page 46)

3 tablespoons honey

⅔ cup Chicken Bone Broth (page 44) or water

1 teaspoon garlic powder

2 tablespoons coconut oil

⅓ cup dry roasted, unsalted almonds, chopped

4 green onions, sliced, for garnish

1. Make the marinade: In a large bowl, whisk together the vinegar, coconut aminos, sesame oil, and tapioca flour. Add the chicken cubes and toss to coat. Cover and place in the refrigerator to marinate for 30 minutes.

2. Make the sauce: In a small bowl, whisk together the coconut aminos, vinegar, toasted sesame oil, tapioca flour, hot sauce, honey, broth, and garlic powder. Set aside.

3. Remove the chicken from the refrigerator and set aside.

4. In a skillet over medium-high heat, melt the coconut oil. Add the chicken and the marinade to the pan and cook for 6 to 8 minutes, until the chicken is no longer pink.

5. Add the sauce, stir, and bring to a boil. Reduce the heat to medium and let simmer for 5 minutes.

6. Add the almonds and stir with a spoon. Let cook for another 2 minutes.

7. Place on four serving plates and garnish with the green onions. Serve immediately.

Chicken Enchilada Casserole

If there's any dish that makes me wish I had two stomachs, it's this one. Homemade enchilada sauce makes the store-bought variety seem like a sad thing that should be used only in case of emergency. I also have a major weakness for casseroles, and with its rich, tomato-y sauce and combination of kale, garlic, and onions, this bad boy hits all my buttons.

PREP TIME · COOK TIME · MAKES

20 min · 55 min · 6 servings

INGREDIENTS

4 Grain-Free Wraps (page 78)

Enchilada sauce

¼ cup bacon fat or lard

1 teaspoon tapioca flour

¼ cup California chili powder (see Note)

1 (6-ounce) can tomato paste

1½ cups Chicken Bone Broth (page 44)

½ teaspoon ground cumin

½ teaspoon sea salt

Filling

1 tablespoon coconut oil

1 small yellow onion, diced

2 cloves garlic, chopped

1 pound boneless, skinless chicken thighs, cut into 1-inch cubes

½ teaspoon dried oregano leaves

¼ teaspoon sea salt

¼ teaspoon ground black pepper

1 (2¼-ounce) can sliced black olives, divided

2 cups packed kale, washed and cut into bite-sized pieces, divided

1. If you don't have leftover wraps on hand, make them and set them aside.

2. Make the enchilada sauce: Place the bacon fat and tapioca flour in a medium saucepan over medium-high heat. Cook until the tapioca flour starts to sizzle.

3. Add the chili powder, tomato paste, broth, cumin, and salt and whisk to combine. Decrease the heat, cover, and let simmer for 10 minutes, then remove from the heat and set aside.

4. Make the filling: In a cast-iron skillet over medium heat, melt the coconut oil. Add the onion and garlic and cook until the onion is translucent, roughly 5 minutes.

5. Add the chicken, oregano, salt, and pepper and mix well. Cook until the chicken is no longer pink, roughly 8 to 10 minutes. Remove from the heat.

6. Preheat the oven to 350°F.

7. In an 8-inch square baking dish, layer as follows: half of the chicken filling, half of the olives, half of the kale, one-third of the enchilada sauce, and then two grain-free wraps. Repeat to create a second layer and then top with the rest of the enchilada sauce.

8. Bake for 30 minutes, or until bubbly and lightly browned on top. Remove from the oven and let cool for 5 minutes before serving.

NOTE: California chili powder is made from Anaheim chiles (also known as New Mexico peppers and California chiles), which have a sweet, pungent, and earthy flavor. California chili powder is available at Mexican and Latin American markets or online from Amazon.

Chicken Pot Pie

Chicken pot pie is the ultimate comfort food. Rich gravy mixed with spices and chicken and topped with a tasty crust will always get my butt to the table. The minute that leaves start to change color in the fall, I have this dish in my oven. Prepare a crust ahead of time to make it an easy weeknight meal.

PREP TIME | COOK TIME | MAKES

 20 min 45 min 6 servings

plus 10 min for the pie crust

INGREDIENTS

Filling

1 tablespoon coconut oil

1 small yellow onion, diced

1 pound boneless, skinless chicken breasts, cut into 1-inch cubes

1 (10-ounce) bag frozen mixed veggies

2 stalks celery, diced

1 teaspoon sea salt

½ teaspoon ground black pepper

½ teaspoon poultry seasoning

¼ teaspoon cayenne pepper

1 tablespoon coconut flour

1½ cups Chicken Bone Broth (page 44)

1 batch Basic Pie Crust dough (page 82), unbaked

1 teaspoon melted coconut oil, for brushing the crust

1. Preheat the oven to 350°F.

2. Make the filling: Melt the coconut oil in a skillet. Add the onion and chicken and cook for 3 to 5 minutes, until the onion has softened and most of the chicken is cooked.

3. Add the mixed veggies, celery, salt, pepper, poultry seasoning, and cayenne pepper and cook for 8 to 10 minutes, until the vegetables are soft and all of the chicken is no longer pink.

4. Add the coconut flour and broth and mix with a spoon until everything is well coated. Spoon the filling into an 8-inch pie pan.

5. Lay the pie crust dough over the filling. Trim off any overhang and crimp the edge to seal. Cut a few vent holes in the crust.

6. Place the pie pan on a rimmed baking sheet to catch any drips and bake for 30 minutes. Take it out of the oven and brush the crust with the melted coconut oil, then return it to the oven and bake for another 5 minutes, until golden.

Sweet-and-Sour Meatballs

My mother catered my wedding, and this was one of the recipes she served. It was lip-smacking delicious, and all I could think was, why the heck didn't she make this for me when I was growing up? Yeah. That was the only time that I turned into a bridezilla during the whole affair, but I did get her recipe, which I then adapted into this tasty dish. The sweet pineapple makes it taste like the traditional recipe you remember. You can serve these meatballs as an appetizer, skewered with toothpicks (just make the meatballs ½ inch in diameter), or over Garlic Fried Rice (page 180) for a complete meal.

PREP TIME   COOK TIME   MAKES

15 min   40 min   4 servings

INGREDIENTS

1 batch Sweet-and-Sour Sauce (page 32)

1 pound ground pork

¼ teaspoon sea salt

½ teaspoon garlic powder

½ teaspoon ginger powder

¼ teaspoon ground black pepper

1 teaspoon tapioca flour

1 teaspoon coconut aminos

1 tablespoon coconut oil, for frying

1 batch Garlic Fried Rice (page 180), for serving (optional)

1. If you are making sweet-and-sour sauce especially for this dish, you can skip the step of cooking it. Simply purée the uncooked sauce and set aside.

2. Place the meat in a large bowl. Add the salt, spices, tapioca flour, and coconut aminos and blend well. Roll the mixture into 1-inch balls and set aside.

3. Melt the coconut oil in a large skillet over medium-high heat.

4. Place the meatballs in the skillet and cook until browned on all sides, roughly 10 minutes.

5. Add the sweet-and-sour sauce and let simmer, uncovered, for 20 minutes. If using puréed, uncooked sauce, let it simmer for an additional 10 minutes. Serve over the fried rice, if desired.

Easy Yellow Curry

The thick, rich coconut milk and curry powder make this dish surprisingly flavorful, but it's still quick and easy to make. It pairs well with Garlic Fried Rice (page 180).

PREP TIME

15 min

COOK TIME
30 min

MAKES
4 servings

INGREDIENTS

1 tablespoon coconut oil

1 small yellow onion, diced

1 pound boneless, skinless chicken breasts, cut into 1-inch cubes

1 (13½-ounce) can full-fat coconut milk

2 tablespoons curry powder

½ teaspoon sea salt

1 teaspoon fish sauce

2 large carrots, peeled and cut into slices ¼ inch thick

1 medium crookneck squash or yellow summer squash, peeled and cut into slices ¼ inch thick

1 green onion, sliced, for garnish (optional)

1. In a large skillet over medium-high heat, melt the coconut oil. Add the onion and cook until translucent, roughly 4 minutes.

2. Add the chicken cubes and cook until the meat is no longer pink, roughly 8 to 10 minutes.

3. Add the coconut milk, curry powder, salt, fish sauce, carrots, and squash and stir to combine.

4. Reduce the heat to medium and let simmer, uncovered, for 15 minutes, until the carrots are fork-tender.

5. Remove from the heat and garnish with the green onion, if desired, before serving.

Salisbury Steak

What is it about Salisbury steak that makes me want to put on a fancy dress and speak with a British accent? Really, it's just fancy hamburger, but oh, mama, is it good. I love mine over Mashed "Potatoes" (page 178), with Creamy Caesar Salad (page 198) on the side.

PREP TIME	COOK TIME	MAKES
20 min	1 hour	4 servings

INGREDIENTS

1 tablespoon coconut oil

2 small yellow onions, diced

1 pound ground beef (85% lean)

½ teaspoon sea salt

¼ teaspoon ground black pepper

2 tablespoons coconut flour

1 cup Chicken Bone Broth (page 44)

1 teaspoon tapioca flour

2 tablespoons tomato paste

2 teaspoons Worcestershire sauce

1. In a skillet over medium-low heat, melt the coconut oil. Add the onions and cook on low, stirring every 10 minutes or so, until the onions are caramelized, about 30 minutes. Set aside.

2. In large bowl, combine the ground beef, salt, pepper, and coconut flour. Add the caramelized onions and mix well. Form into four 4-inch patties.

3. Preheat a dry skillet over medium-high heat and set the patties in the pan. Cook for 4 to 6 minutes per side.

4. In a small bowl, combine the broth, tapioca flour, tomato paste, and Worcestershire sauce. Whisk to combine.

5. Pour the sauce into the skillet and decrease the heat to medium-low. Cover and cook for 15 to 20 minutes, until the sauce has thickened into a gravy.

Oven-Baked Chicken Balls

These chicken balls are among my favorite foods in this book. They have a wonderful peppery taste, and the combination of onions, celery, and spices reminds my husband of the holidays. They go well with Mashed "Potatoes" (page 178) and Honey Ginger Carrots (page 186) for a complete meal, but you can also serve them skewered with toothpicks for an appetizer—just make them ½ inch in diameter and reduce the baking time to 15 to 18 minutes.

PREP TIME   COOK TIME   MAKES

 10 min   25 min   4 servings

INGREDIENTS

1 small yellow onion, diced

1 (4-ounce) bag plain plantain chips, crushed

1 pound ground chicken (see Note)

½ teaspoon sea salt

1 tablespoon dried cilantro leaves

½ teaspoon garlic powder

½ teaspoon ginger powder

½ teaspoon ground black pepper

Ketchup (page 28), for serving (optional)

1. Preheat the oven to 365°F. Line a rimmed baking sheet with parchment paper.

2. In a small bowl, combine the onion, crushed plantain chips, ground chicken, salt, and spices and mix until well combined. Shape the mixture into 2-inch balls.

3. Place the balls on the prepared baking sheet and bake for 20 to 25 minutes. Halfway through baking, turn the balls so that the other side gets nicely browned.

4. Remove from the oven and serve immediately with homemade ketchup on the side for dipping, if desired.

NOTE: If you can't find ground chicken in your grocery store, it's easy to make at home. Simply cut 1 pound of boneless, skinless chicken breasts or thighs into 2-inch chunks, place in a food processor, and pulse. Do not set the machine on automatic; just pulse until you get the right texture. For me, that's about 15 pulses. Voilà—easy peasy.

Roasted Chicken

Everyone loves bacon, and the saved drippings make a delicious coating for roasted poultry and meats. Here, the combination of bacon fat, garlic, thyme, and rosemary turns an average roasted chicken into a moist, perfectly seasoned bird. The recipe is beyond simple, yet it packs a punch of flavor. Don't forget to save the carcass to make Chicken Bone Broth (page 44).

PREP TIME

15 min
plus 10 min to rest

COOK TIME

2 hours

MAKES
4 servings

INGREDIENTS

1 teaspoon sea salt

½ teaspoon dried crushed rosemary

½ teaspoon dried thyme

½ teaspoon ground black pepper

½ teaspoon garlic powder

⅓ cup bacon fat, softened but still solid

1 (5-pound) whole chicken, at room temperature

1. Preheat the oven to 375°F.

2. In a small bowl, combine the salt, spices, and bacon fat. Stir to distribute the seasonings throughout the fat.

3. Gently spread 2 tablespoons of the seasoned fat underneath the chicken skin on the breast area. Spread the remainder all over the outside of the chicken.

4. Place the chicken breast side up in a large cast-iron skillet and roast for 2 hours, or until a thermometer inserted in the inner thigh reads 165°F (see Note).

5. Remove from the oven and let sit for 10 minutes before carving.

NOTE: The cooking time in this recipe is based on using a 5-pound bird. If your chicken weighs more or less, adjust the cooking time using this formula: 20 minutes per pound plus an extra 20 minutes.

Roasted Turkey

Who can resist a golden bird that has been smothered in bacon fat and whose every bite is perfectly moist? Some proclaim that you have to brine a turkey for it to be moist and tasty, but I don't have the room or equipment for that. This recipe gives you an equally delicious, juicy bird—and it's much easier to make. When planning, remember to allow time for the turkey to defrost completely in the refrigerator (see chart).

PREP TIME 10 min

plus 1 hour 20 min to rest

COOK TIME 2⅓ hours

MAKES 6 servings

INGREDIENTS

1 (11-pound) whole turkey, fully defrosted (see chart below)

1 teaspoon sea salt

½ teaspoon dried crushed rosemary

½ teaspoon dried thyme

½ teaspoon ground black pepper

½ teaspoon garlic powder

⅓ cup bacon fat, softened but still solid

2 cups Chicken Bone Broth (page 44)

NOTE: The standard roasting time for an unstuffed turkey is 13 minutes per pound, which is what I've used here. Please note that if you stuff the turkey, you will need to increase the roasting time by 1 to 1½ hours to reach an internal temperature of 165°F.

1. Wash the thawed turkey and remove the giblets and neck, then let it sit out on the counter for 1 hour before roasting.

2. Preheat the oven to 375°F. Place a rack inside a roasting pan.

3. In a small bowl, combine the salt, spices, and bacon fat and stir to blend the seasonings into the fat.

4. Gently spread 3 tablespoons of the seasoned fat underneath the turkey skin on the breast area. Spread the remainder all over the outside of the turkey. If you have any fat left over after coating the outside, place it in the cavity.

5. Set the turkey breast side up on the roasting rack and pour the chicken broth in the bottom of the roasting pan. Roast, uncovered, for a total of 2 hours 20 minutes, or until the temperature of the inner thigh is 165°F. After 1 hour, tent the breast area with foil and then continue to roast. After 1 hour 50 minutes, check the temperature to make sure you don't overcook the turkey. Optionally, for even browning, you may baste the turkey every 35 minutes.

6. Remove from the oven and let sit for 20 minutes before carving.

How long will it take to defrost a turkey in the fridge?

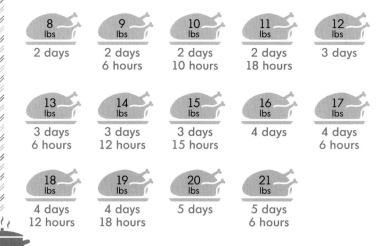

8 lbs	9 lbs	10 lbs	11 lbs	12 lbs
2 days	2 days 6 hours	2 days 10 hours	2 days 18 hours	3 days

13 lbs	14 lbs	15 lbs	16 lbs	17 lbs
3 days 6 hours	3 days 12 hours	3 days 15 hours	4 days	4 days 6 hours

18 lbs	19 lbs	20 lbs	21 lbs
4 days 12 hours	4 days 18 hours	5 days	5 days 6 hours

Clam Chowder

When we lived in St. Johns, a small neighborhood in Portland, Oregon, my husband and I used to go to a tiny fish restaurant that served the most amazing clam chowder. I cried big baby tears when I discovered that most clam chowder recipes are packed with flour and dairy, and I decided I had to create my own Paleo-friendly version. This recipe uses cauliflower to create that famous creamy broth with none of the harmful gluten or dairy. For the perfect comfort meal, serve it with Garlic Bread Rolls (page 90).

PREP TIME **20** min   COOK TIME **30** min   MAKES **4** servings

INGREDIENTS

1 small head cauliflower, cored and roughly chopped

6 strips bacon, diced

½ medium yellow onion, diced

2 stalks celery, diced

2 cups Chicken Bone Broth (page 44)

1 tablespoon tapioca flour

1 pound chopped clams with broth

½ teaspoon apple cider vinegar

1 bay leaf

½ teaspoon dried thyme leaves

½ teaspoon sea salt

½ teaspoon ground black pepper

fresh or dried thyme, for garnish

1. Place the chopped cauliflower in a large pot and cover with water. Bring to a boil over medium-high heat and cook for 10 minutes, until completely softened.

2. Meanwhile, in a large saucepan over medium-high heat, sauté the bacon, onion, and celery until the onion is translucent, 3 to 5 minutes.

3. Drain the cooked cauliflower. Place in a blender with the broth and tapioca flour and blend until completely smooth.

4. Add the puréed cauliflower to the saucepan with the bacon along with the clams, vinegar, bay leaf, thyme leaves, salt, and pepper. Stir well and cook for 20 minutes over medium heat.

5. Remove from the heat, garnish with fresh or dried thyme leaves, and serve.

Chicken and Dumplings

I can still perfectly recall my mother working on chicken and dumplings on a cold November morning: I can see the light hitting her face and hear the sound of the thick gravy bubbling, interrupted only by the soft pop of the dumplings being dropped into all that deliciousness. The blend of almond flour and tapioca flour in this recipe makes for the perfect dumpling, both light and slightly soft in the middle. This dish will have you asking for seconds—I promise!

PREP TIME COOK TIME MAKES

15 min | 1⅓ hours | 6 servings

INGREDIENTS

Broth

3 pounds bone-in, skin-on chicken thighs

1 small yellow onion, diced

2 stalks celery, diced

6 cups water

1½ teaspoons poultry seasoning

1 teaspoon sea salt

½ cup canned, full-fat coconut milk

2 tablespoons tapioca flour

Dumplings

1½ cups blanched, superfine almond flour

½ cup tapioca flour

½ teaspoon sea salt

⅓ cup broth (from above)

2 tablespoons chopped fresh curly parsley, for garnish

1. Make the broth: Place the chicken thighs, onion, celery, water, poultry seasoning, and salt in a soup pot. Cover and cook over medium heat for 1 hour.

2. Reduce the heat to low and remove the chicken thighs from the broth. Remove the meat from the bones and place the meat back in the soup.

3. In a small cup, mix the coconut milk and the tapioca flour with a fork to make a slurry.

4. Pour the slurry into the soup and mix until well blended.

5. Make the dumplings: Mix the almond flour, tapioca flour, and salt in a small bowl.

6. Pour ⅓ cup of the broth into the flours and salt and mix until you have a soft dough.

7. Using your hands, roll the dough into small balls. You should get twelve dumplings.

8. Drop the dumplings into the simmering broth and cook for 15 minutes over medium-low heat.

9. Remove from the heat, ladle into bowls, garnish with the parsley, and serve.

Pierogi

It seems like a majority of my food discoveries happened in college. My roommate, Liz, introduced me to pierogi, and pretty soon I couldn't go a day without whipping up a batch and smothering them in butter. I was a pierogi addict. The crust used here is firmer than traditional pierogi, but oh, man, these take me back. The combination of sweet potato and fennel seeds makes for a flavorful treat you won't soon forget.

PREP TIME COOK TIME MAKES

20 min   30 min   10 pierogi

plus 15 min for the pie crusts and 20 min for the sweet potato

INGREDIENTS

Filling

1 tablespoon coconut oil

½ small yellow onion, diced

1 cup mashed sweet potato (1 small sweet potato; see Note, page 80)

½ teaspoon sea salt

½ teaspoon fennel seeds

¼ teaspoon ground black pepper

2 batches Basic Pie Crust dough (page 82), unbaked

1. Preheat the oven to 350°F. Line a baking sheet with parchment paper.

2. Making the filling: In a skillet over medium-high heat, melt the coconut oil. Add the onion and sauté for 4 to 5 minutes, until the onion is translucent.

3. Add the sweet potato, salt, fennel, and pepper and stir until well combined. Remove from the heat and set aside.

4. Prepare the dough: After kneading, roll out the pie crust dough between two sheets of parchment paper to a 10-inch square that is ¼ to ½ inch thick. With a large cookie cutter or cup, cut out 20 circles.

5. Place 1 tablespoon of the filling in the center of a dough circle. Set another circle on top and lightly pinch the edges to close. The dough may crack slightly; if it does, you can close the seams with a drop of water.

6. Place the pierogi on the prepared baking sheet and repeat with the remaining dough circles and filling.

7. Bake for 20 to 25 minutes, until golden brown.

8. Remove from the oven and let cool on the pan for 5 minutes before serving.

Creamy Chicken and Broccolini Bake

Casseroles are one of my favorite things to cook, mostly because they are easy to make and there are always leftovers. Here, a flavorful creamy sauce smothers the chicken and broccolini, making for a lip-smacking dinner. You will lick the spoon!

PREP TIME	COOK TIME	MAKES
15 min	30 min	6 servings

INGREDIENTS

2 tablespoons coconut oil, plus more for greasing the baking dish

2 bunches broccolini, stemmed and chopped into florets

1½ to 2 pounds boneless, skinless chicken breasts, cut into 1-inch cubes

½ large yellow onion, diced

2 (13½-ounce) cans full-fat coconut milk, chilled overnight

5 cloves garlic, minced

½ cup Chicken Bone Broth (page 44)

1 tablespoon tapioca flour

½ teaspoon sea salt

½ teaspoon red pepper flakes

½ teaspoon poultry seasoning

¼ teaspoon ground black pepper

1. Preheat the oven to 350°F. Grease a 7-by-11-inch baking dish.

2. Create an even layer of the broccolini on the bottom of the prepared baking dish.

3. In a skillet over medium-high heat, melt the coconut oil. Add the chicken and onion and cook until the chicken is no longer pink, roughly 10 to 12 minutes.

4. Open the cans of coconut milk and carefully scoop the solid coconut cream from the top. (You can save the leftover water and use it in smoothies.)

5. Add the coconut cream, garlic, broth, tapioca flour, salt, and spices to the skillet and mix with a fork until well combined. Let simmer over medium heat to allow the flavors to meld, about 5 minutes.

6. Pour the chicken and sauce over the broccolini and bake for 15 minutes, until light golden brown on top.

CHAPTER 5

SIDES & SALADS

Cranberry Sauce

Homemade cranberry sauce is insanely simple to make, and it's a pretty impressive thing to have on the holiday dinner table. I love the scent and taste of cinnamon in this recipe. If this sauce is too tart for your taste buds, you can easily increase the honey.

PREP TIME
5 min

plus 4 hours to chill

COOK TIME
20 min

MAKES
6
servings

INGREDIENTS

12 ounces **fresh cranberries**

2 cups **frozen or fresh pitted cherries**

⅓ cup **honey**

⅓ cup **water**

1 teaspoon **ground cinnamon**

DIET

AIP

OCCASION

Holiday

1. In a large saucepan, combine all of the ingredients and mix with a spoon. Bring to a boil over medium heat.

2. Lower the heat and let simmer, uncovered, for 15 minutes, or until most of the cranberries have popped. For a smoother sauce, you can use a potato masher to crush the cherries or use a fork to help break them up. Remove from the heat and let cool to room temperature.

3. Pour the sauce into an airtight container and chill in the refrigerator for 4 hours before serving.

4. This sauce will keep in the fridge for up to a week.

Creamy Cucumber Dill Salad

This is my go-to salad for summer. It makes the perfect cool, creamy side dish for lunch or dinner, and it's so tasty, no one will ever know how healthy it is. It's great with Oven-Baked Dry-Rubbed Ribs (page 120), Southern Fried Chicken (page 138), and Lamb Gyro Burgers (page 140), or even as a topping for Sloppy Joes (page 128).

PREP TIME

15 min

MAKES

6 servings

plus 1 hour to chill

INGREDIENTS

3 large cucumbers, cut into slices ¼ inch thick

½ teaspoon sea salt

Dressing

½ cup Homemade Mayo (page 30)

¼ cup canned, full-fat coconut milk

1 teaspoon dried dill weed

½ teaspoon garlic powder

¼ teaspoon sea salt

½ teaspoon apple cider vinegar

1. Place the cucumber slices in a medium bowl, toss with the salt, and set aside.

2. In a small bowl, combine the ingredients for the dressing and whisk until smooth.

3. Pour the dressing over the cucumbers and toss to coat evenly.

4. Place the bowl in the refrigerator to chill for 1 hour before serving.

Mashed "Potatoes"

Cauliflower is the perfect substitute for potatoes, and with this seasoning you won't even know that you're eating something healthier—the bacon fat gives this dish an incredible flavor that is a rocking good time for your taste buds. The trick to making this dish the perfect stand-in for mashed white potatoes is puréeing the cauliflower until smooth. I can't have Meatloaf (page 122) or Southern Fried Chicken (page 138) without it.

PREP TIME COOK TIME MAKES
10 min · 10 min · 4 servings

INGREDIENTS

1 medium head cauliflower (2 pounds), cored and roughly chopped

4 cups water

2 tablespoons melted bacon fat

½ cup canned, full-fat coconut milk

½ teaspoon sea salt

½ teaspoon garlic powder

¼ teaspoon dried thyme leaves

¼ teaspoon ground nutmeg

OCCASION

Holiday

1. Place the cauliflower and water in a large saucepan. Bring to a boil over medium heat and cook for 8 to 10 minutes.

2. Drain the cauliflower and place in a food processor with the bacon fat, coconut milk, salt, garlic powder, thyme, and nutmeg. Pulse until smooth.

Garlic Fried Rice

With my Filipino roots, I grew up eating garlic fried rice with spicy sausage links for breakfast. It was heavenly, and I begged my mom to make it every day, even passing up pancakes or French toast for this dish. I'm so glad that I can still enjoy it on the Paleo diet, with a twist—cauliflower replaces the white rice. Garlic is my hands-down favorite pungent spice, so I use a lot (even more than my mom). But you can easily reduce the number of cloves in this recipe if the flavor is too strong for you.

PREP TIME   COOK TIME   MAKES

10 min   **20** min   **4** servings

INGREDIENTS

1 medium head cauliflower (2 pounds), cored and roughly chopped

3 tablespoons coconut oil, divided

8 cloves garlic, minced

¾ teaspoon sea salt, divided

½ teaspoon ground black pepper

3 large eggs

1. Place the cauliflower in a food processor and pulse until chopped into pieces the size of grains of rice. Set aside.

2. In a large skillet over medium-high heat, melt 2 tablespoons of the coconut oil. Add the minced garlic and sauté for 3 to 4 minutes. Add the cauliflower and season with ½ teaspoon of the salt and the pepper. Mix well and cook for 8 to 10 minutes, until some of the "rice" is light golden brown.

3. In a small bowl, whisk the eggs with the remaining ¼ teaspoon of salt.

4. Push the cooked cauliflower to the sides of the pan to make a large well in the middle of the skillet. Melt the remaining 1 tablespoon of coconut oil in the well.

5. Pour in the beaten eggs and push them around the center of the pan with a heat-resistant spatula to scramble them.

6. When cooked to your liking, mix the eggs and cauliflower rice together and serve immediately.

Hush Puppies

When I was a kid, once a week my parents packed us up, took us to the nearest fish-fry chain restaurant, and filled us up with battered fried fish and hush puppies. I knew that I had to re-create a Paleo version of these puppies so that I could share with my son the magic of deep-fried foods done right. This recipe is also pretty adaptable. You can easily add sausage, green chiles, or shrimp to make it your own.

PREP TIME
10 min

COOK TIME
15 min

MAKES
14 hush puppies

INGREDIENTS

½ large yellow onion

1 large egg

½ teaspoon apple cider vinegar

1 tablespoon honey

½ teaspoon baking soda

½ teaspoon baking powder

½ teaspoon sea salt

1½ cups blanched, superfine almond flour

¼ cup coconut flour

4 cups coconut oil, for frying

1. In a food processor, pulse the onion until completely minced.

2. Add the egg, vinegar, honey, baking soda, baking powder, salt, almond flour, and coconut flour. Pulse until a dough forms, roughly 30 seconds.

3. In a Dutch oven over medium-high heat, heat the coconut oil to 365°F.

4. Scoop out a portion of dough with a large spoon and roll it into a 2-inch ball. Set on a piece of parchment paper and repeat until all of the dough has been formed into balls.

5. Drop four hush puppies at a time into the hot oil and let brown on one side, about 2½ minutes. Flip and brown on the other side, about 2½ minutes.

6. Using a slotted spoon, remove the hush puppies from the oil and set on a paper towel to drain. Repeat until all of the hush puppies are cooked. Serve immediately.

Bucha Onion Rings

Light, crispy, and addictive, these are ideal for a Super Bowl party, or any time you feel the hankering for some deep-fried goodness. Inspired by classic beer-battered onion rings, this recipe uses grain-free kombucha instead of beer, but they taste exactly the same. Homemade Ketchup (page 28) is the perfect accompaniment.

PREP TIME 15 min   COOK TIME 24 min   MAKES 4 servings

INGREDIENTS

1 large vidala onion, peeled and cut into slices ¼ inch thick

¼ cup tapioca flour

Batter

¾ cup tapioca flour

½ cup blanched, superfine almond flour

1 teaspoon sea salt

½ teaspoon garlic powder

½ teaspoon ground black pepper

½ cup plain kombucha

4 cups coconut oil, for frying

OCCASION

Game day

1. Separate the onion rings, place them in a bowl, and toss them with the ¼ cup of tapioca flour until evenly coated. Set aside.

2. Make the batter: In a second large bowl, combine the tapioca flour, almond flour, salt, garlic powder, and pepper and mix well with spoon.

3. Pour in the kombucha and stir until you have a thick batter. Let the batter sit for 10 minutes.

4. In a Dutch oven over medium-high heat, heat the oil to 350°F.

5. Dip one of the onion rings in the batter until well coated, then gently drop it into the hot oil. Repeat with three or four additional rings, without overcrowding the pan. Let the rings fry until golden brown on one side, 3 to 4 minutes. Flip and repeat.

6. Using tongs, remove the onion rings and set on a paper towel to drain. Repeat with the rest of the onion rings and batter until all are fried.

Honey Ginger Carrots

I think a bunch of carrots is almost as pretty as a bouquet of flowers, but it makes a better gift: One, you can eat the tops (though since they're pretty bitter, they should be used sparingly in salads); and two, when cooked this way, carrots are a sweet treat. The combination of honey, ginger, and carrots tastes like fall, and this quick side dish pairs well with Salisbury Steak (page 156), Meatloaf (page 122), Oven-Baked Chicken Balls (page 158), and Roasted Chicken (page 160).

PREP TIME
10 min

COOK TIME
10 min

MAKES
4
servings

INGREDIENTS

¼ cup Chicken Bone Broth (page 44)

1 teaspoon honey

½ teaspoon sea salt

2 tablespoons coconut oil

1 tablespoon minced ginger

4 large carrots, peeled and cut into ¼-inch-thick rounds

DIET

AIP

1. In a skillet over medium-low heat, combine the broth, honey, salt, coconut oil, and ginger and mix with a spoon until well blended. Add the carrots and cook for 8 to 10 minutes, until tender but still firm.

2. Remove from the heat and serve immediately.

Creamed Brussels Sprouts

This is the only way to eat Brussels sprouts: cooked in rich, creamy fat and seasoned correctly. There's a world of difference between these and the bitter sprouts I ate as a child, steamed and spritzed with lemon juice. Even sprouts haters will love these. In fact, thanks to this dish, Brussels sprouts are my two-year-old son's favorite vegetable.

PREP TIME 10 min

COOK TIME 25 min

MAKES 3 servings

INGREDIENTS

1 pound Brussels sprouts

1 (13½-ounce) can full-fat coconut milk, chilled overnight

2 tablespoons coconut oil

½ teaspoon sea salt

½ teaspoon ground black pepper

DIET

 AIP

1. Bring a pot of water to a boil.

2. Cut off the brown ends of the Brussels sprouts and pull off any yellowed outer leaves. Slice the sprouts in half.

3. Drop the Brussels sprouts into the boiling water and cook for 10 minutes to soften. Drain and set aside until cool enough to handle.

4. Open the can of coconut milk and carefully scoop out the solid coconut cream that has risen to the top. Set this cream aside. (You can use the leftover coconut water in smoothies.)

5. In a large skillet over medium-high heat, melt the coconut oil. Place the Brussels sprouts cut side down in the skillet. Let them brown undisturbed, roughly 8 minutes.

6. Flip the sprouts and season with the salt and pepper. Stir with a heat-resistant spatula and cook for 3 minutes.

7. Add the coconut cream and stir to evenly coat the Brussels sprouts. Let simmer for 2 more minutes to allow the cream to thicken. Serve immediately.

Rosemary Garlic Summer Squash

Though this recipe is simple, the rosemary and garlic pack a punch of flavor. Looking at it, you might wonder what the fuss is all about, but don't let the photo fool you: this is one tasty dish that will put a surprised smile on your face. I make this when I want a quick, no-fuss side dish to serve with dinner.

PREP TIME
10 min

COOK TIME
8 min

MAKES
4 servings

INGREDIENTS

2 tablespoons coconut oil

2 large crookneck squash or yellow summer squash, cut into ¼-inch-thick slices

½ teaspoon dried crushed rosemary

¼ teaspoon garlic powder

¼ teaspoon sea salt

DIET

In a skillet over medium-low heat, melt the coconut oil. Add the sliced squash, sprinkle with the spices and salt, and mix well. Cook for 5 to 8 minutes, until the squash is slightly soft. Serve immediately.

Duchess Sweet Potatoes

Duchess sweet potatoes are almost too cute to eat when piped into fancy mounds. The warmth of the sweet potatoes and spice of the nutmeg create a flavor that reminds me so much of the holidays that it always makes me want to turn on Christmas music and bust out my red snowman sweater.

PREP TIME   COOK TIME   MAKES

15 min

30 min

6 servings

INGREDIENTS

2 pounds sweet potatoes, peeled and cut into 1-inch cubes

1 (13½-ounce) can full-fat coconut milk, chilled overnight

½ teaspoon sea salt

½ teaspoon ground nutmeg

¼ teaspoon ground black pepper

2 large egg yolks

1 tablespoon coconut oil, melted

OCCASION

Holiday

1. Preheat the oven to 350°F. Line a baking sheet with parchment paper.

2. Place the sweet potatoes in a large saucepan and fill it with enough water to cover them by 1 inch. Bring to a boil over medium-high heat, then lower the heat to medium and let simmer until the potatoes are soft, roughly 10 minutes. Drain the potatoes and set in a large bowl to cool.

3. Open the can of coconut milk and carefully scoop out the solid coconut cream that has risen to the top. (You can use the leftover coconut water in smoothies.) Place the cream in the bowl with the cooked sweet potatoes.

4. To the bowl, add the salt, nutmeg, pepper, egg yolks, and coconut oil and mash with a potato masher until well blended and smooth.

5. Place the sweet potatoes in a piping bag fitted with a star tip (see Note). Pipe into 2-inch-wide pyramids on the prepared baking sheet.

6. Continue piping until all of the mixture is gone.

7. Bake for 18 to 20 minutes, until lightly browned on top.

NOTE: If you don't have a piping bag, you can use a plastic food storage bag instead. Fill the bag with the potato mixture, cut a small triangle off of one corner, and then pipe away.

Spinach Nuggets

Packed full of spinach and spices, these nuggets remind me of the pizzas my mother made every Saturday when I was growing up, with puréed spinach mixed into the dough. Not only was the dough green, which we thought was very cool, mixing the spinach with the dough also solved our problems with the texture of cooked spinach. These fun, bite-sized treats are similar to cookies, and they're great to send along in your kids lunchboxes. They'll never know they're eating healthy!

PREP TIME	COOK TIME	MAKES
10 min	18 min	12 nuggets

INGREDIENTS

1 small yellow onion, peeled

2 cups packed spinach leaves

1¼ cups blanched, superfine almond flour

½ teaspoon sea salt

½ teaspoon ground black pepper

½ teaspoon garlic powder

½ teaspoon dried oregano leaves

½ teaspoon dried basil leaves

¼ teaspoon fennel seeds

1 large egg

1. Preheat the oven to 350°F. Line a rimmed baking sheet with parchment paper.

2. Place the onion in a food processor and pulse until minced. Add the spinach, almond flour, salt, spices, and egg and pulse until you have a batter.

3. Drop the batter by the spoonful onto the prepared baking sheet.

4. Bake for 15 to 18 minutes, until a toothpick inserted into the middle of a nugget comes out clean.

5. Remove from the oven and let cool for 5 minutes before serving.

NOTE: If you're not a fan of the flavor of licorice, omit the fennel and you'll still have a tasty, kid-friendly treat.

Sweet Potato Salad

Something about the combination of sweet potatoes and mayo always gets me breaking out my sunscreen and looking for a tiny ray of sunshine, ready for barbecues and beach parties. I'm pretty sure that sweet potato salad is a mandatory dish at all those summertime events, and the creamy dill dressing and capers used in this recipe make it amazing. This dish pairs well with Southern Fried Chicken (page 138) and Oven-Baked Dry-Rubbed Ribs (page 120).

PREP TIME

20
min

COOK TIME

15
min

MAKES
6
servings

plus 2 hours to chill

INGREDIENTS

2 pounds sweet potatoes, peeled and cut into ½-inch dice

Dressing

2 large pastured egg yolks

1 tablespoon lemon juice

1 tablespoon apple cider vinegar

1 teaspoon honey

1 teaspoon sea salt

½ teaspoon ground black pepper

½ teaspoon dried dill weed

¾ cup light olive oil

1 small yellow onion, diced

2 stalks celery, diced

1 teaspoon capers

OCCASION

Game day

1. Fill a large stockpot halfway with water and bring to a boil. Add the diced sweet potatoes and cook for 10 to 15 minutes, until soft. Drain and let cool completely.

2. While the sweet potatoes are cooking, make the dressing: In a blender, combine all of the ingredients for the dressing except the olive oil and blend until smooth. Turn the blender to its lowest setting and slowly drizzle in the olive oil. Continue until all of the oil is gone and then blend until the dressing reaches a thick, creamy consistency.

3. Place the cooled sweet potatoes in a bowl along with the onion, celery, and capers. Pour the dressing over the vegetables and lightly toss with a spoon until fully coated.

4. Place the salad in the refrigerator to chill for at least 2 hours. Overnight is better.

NOTE: If the dressing fails to emulsify, you can set it in the fridge for an hour to thicken.

Creamy Caesar Salad

I ate this salad every single day when I was pregnant with my son. I couldn't get enough of the crisp romaine lettuce paired with the zesty flavor of anchovies and garlic—all wrapped in the velvety texture of mayo. The only downside? You end up with a bad case of garlic breath after eating this dish.

PREP TIME
10 min

MAKES
2
servings

INGREDIENTS

1 small red bell pepper

1 head romaine lettuce, sliced into ½-inch strips

Dressing

2 large pastured egg yolks

1½ teaspoons garlic powder

1 teaspoon sea salt

½ teaspoon ground black pepper

4 ounces anchovy fillets, minced

1 tablespoon lemon juice

1 tablespoon apple cider vinegar

1 cup light olive oil

2 tablespoons pine nuts

2 hard-boiled eggs, diced (optional)

1. Slice the bell pepper in half and remove the seeds. Place half in the fridge for another dish or snack. Cut the remaining half lengthwise into strips and then in half crosswise.

2. In a serving bowl, toss the romaine lettuce with the bell pepper strips. Set aside.

3. Make the dressing: In a blender, combine all of the ingredients for the dressing except the olive oil and blend until smooth. Turn the blender to its lowest setting and slowly drizzle in the olive oil. Continue until all of the oil is gone and then blend until the dressing reaches a thick, creamy consistency.

4. Pour ½ cup of the dressing over the salad and toss to coat. Top with the pine nuts and diced hard-boiled eggs, if desired, and serve immediately.

5. Store the remaining dressing in the fridge for up to a week.

NOTE: If the dressing fails to emulsify, you can set it in the fridge for an hour to thicken.

Braised Red Cabbage and Apples

Cabbage is one of the B-list celebrities of vegetables, right next to celery, but braising it turns it ino a star by softening the bitter flavor. Here, the Granny Smith apples add a nice tart punch. This versatile recipe can be served hot or cold.

PREP TIME
20 min

COOK TIME
1 hour

MAKES
6 servings

INGREDIENTS

4 strips bacon, diced

1 medium yellow onion, diced

2½ pounds red cabbage, halved, cored, and cut into ½-inch strips

½ cup apple cider vinegar

1 cup water

2 tablespoons honey

1 teaspoon sea salt

1 Granny Smith apple, peeled, cored, and cut into ½-inch dice

½ teaspoon ground black pepper

1. In a large skillet over medium-high heat, cook the diced bacon until crispy, roughly 8 minutes.

2. Add the onion and cook, stirring occasionally, until translucent, about 5 minutes.

3. Add the cabbage, vinegar, water, honey, and salt and stir. Cover and cook for 15 minutes.

4. Reduce the heat to medium-low and stir in the apple. Cook, covered, for 30 minutes.

5. Season with the pepper and either serve hot or chill in the refrigerator for 4 hours and serve cold.

6. This dish will keep for 4 to 5 days in an airtight container in the refrigerator.

Thanksgiving Dressing

Dressing, also commonly referred to as stuffing, is my favorite holiday dish. I can't think of Thanksgiving without drooling over the thought of a huge side of this dressing smothered in Mushroom Gravy (page 54) and topped with Cranberry Sauce (page 174). It's enough to make me want to break out my stretchy pants. I highly recommend that you make a double batch, because this recipe is going to disappear before your eyes (into your Aunt Edna's stomach).

PREP TIME COOK TIME MAKES

20 min

1 hour

4 servings

INGREDIENTS

Bread

2 tablespoons unsalted butter or coconut oil, plus more for greasing the pan

2½ cups blanched, superfine almond flour

½ cup tapioca flour

1 teaspoon baking soda

1 teaspoon sea salt

½ teaspoon dried thyme

1 cup Chicken Bone Broth (page 44), plus more if needed

½ teaspoon apple cider vinegar

2 tablespoons melted coconut oil

2 stalks celery, diced

4 slices bacon, diced

1 small yellow onion, diced

OCCASION

Holiday

1. Preheat the oven to 350°F. Grease a 7-by-10-inch baking dish.

2. In a large bowl, combine the ingredients for the bread and blend with a spoon until you have a smooth batter.

3. Pour the batter into the prepared baking dish and bake for 30 minutes, or until light golden brown on top. Remove from the oven and reduce the oven temperature to 300°F.

4. Leaving the bread in the dish, break it up into small pieces with a fork. It should be somewhat sticky. If the mixture is dry, add ½ cup broth.

5. Add the coconut oil, celery, bacon, and onion to the dish and mix thoroughly.

6. Cover with foil or a lid and bake for 30 minutes, or until the bacon is cooked.

NOTE: To make this dish vegan, you can swap out the chicken broth for vegetable broth and omit the bacon.

Green Bean Casserole

Who doesn't love a traditional green bean casserole? It's a dish that's expected on the table for the holidays, and thankfully, making it from scratch isn't as difficult as you might think it would be. The hot, bubbly mushroom gravy will sweep you off your feet, and the crispy onion topping adds a nice crunch that will remind you of the dish you grew up eating.

PREP TIME

15 min

plus 35 min for the gravy

COOK TIME
1¼ hours

MAKES
6 servings

INGREDIENTS

1 batch Mushroom Gravy (page 54)

Crispy onion topping

1 cup coconut oil

1 large yellow onion, halved and sliced into ¼-inch-thick half-moons

2 tablespoons tapioca flour

¼ teaspoon sea salt

Green beans

4 cups water

1¼ pounds fresh green beans, trimmed and cleaned

4 strips bacon, fried until crispy and crumbled

OCCASION

Holiday

1. Have the gravy prepared and ready to go.

2. Preheat the oven to 350°F.

3. Make the crispy onion topping: In a medium saucepan over medium heat, heat the coconut oil to 365°F. In a bowl, combine the onion, tapioca flour, and salt and toss until well coated.

4. Working in batches, gently drop the onion slices into the hot oil and cook until golden brown, 3 to 4 minutes per batch. Set the onion slices on a paper towel to drain.

5. Make the green beans: Bring the water to a boil in a large saucepan. Add the green beans, return the water to a boil, and cook for 10 minutes. Drain the beans.

6. In a 7-by-10-inch casserole dish, combine the green beans, gravy, and crumbled bacon. Stir with a spatula until the beans are well coated.

7. Reserve ½ cup of the fried onions and place the remainder on top of the green bean casserole.

8. Bake for 30 minutes, or until bubbly and light golden brown.

9. Remove from the oven, garnish with the reserved fried onions, and serve immediately.

NOTE: While green beans are legumes, which are avoided on the Paleo diet, they have the lowest levels of phytates, so your body can aborb more of the vitamins.

Hummus

This simple recipe makes the perfect appetizer or snack. I love to eat hummus with Lamb Gyro Burgers (page 140) or spread it in Grain-Free Wraps (page 78) with some veggies for a quick lunch. Like many of my recipes, this hummus will give you a bad case of garlic breath, but you'll have a smile on your face and a full stomach afterward.

PREP TIME   COOK TIME   MAKES

10 min   2 min   4 servings

INGREDIENTS

2 large zucchini, peeled and sliced

¼ cup Tahini Sauce (page 42)

2 tablespoons lemon juice

2 cloves garlic, minced

½ teaspoon sea salt

½ teaspoon ground black pepper

1 tablespoon extra-virgin olive oil, for garnish

¼ teaspoon paprika, for garnish

1 tablespoon roughly chopped fresh parsley, for garnish

1. Bring a large saucepan of water to a boil over medium-high heat. Drop the zucchini slices into the water and cook for 2 minutes. Drain.

2. Place the cooked zucchini in a food processor along with the tahini sauce, lemon juice, garlic, salt, and pepper. Pulse until smooth.

3. Transfer the hummus to a serving bowl and top with the olive oil, paprika, and parsley. You can eat it immediately or chill for an hour before serving.

4. This hummus will keep for 3 to 4 days in an airtight container in the refrigerator.

Creamy Grits

A favorite Southern dish that is divine with eggs, grits makes a great side dish for any meal. Here, the bacon fat and almond meal make this grain-free twist on classic grits taste like the real deal. If you want to make cheese-flavored grits, you can add ½ cup nutritional yeast.

PREP TIME COOK TIME MAKES

10 min

35 min

4 servings

INGREDIENTS

1 small head cauliflower, cored and roughly chopped

2½ cups Chicken Bone Broth (page 44)

1 tablespoon bacon fat

1 tablespoon tapioca flour

1 teaspoon sea salt

1 teaspoon garlic powder

1 cup almond meal

Hot Sauce (page 46), for serving (optional)

1. Place the cauliflower in a food processor and pulse until the pieces are the size of rice. Set aside 3½ cups. You can freeze the rest and use it as needed in other recipes, such as Garlic Fried Rice (page 180).

2. Combine the 3½ cups riced cauliflower and broth in a large skillet. Bring to a boil over medium-high heat.

3. To the skillet, add the bacon fat, tapioca flour, salt, and garlic powder and mix with a heat-resistant spatula until blended. Cook for 12 minutes, stirring occasionally.

4. Add the almond meal, stir, and cook for 15 to 20 minutes, until the texture is somewhat creamy and soft.

5. Remove from the heat and serve immediately with hot sauce, if desired.

Zucchini Noodles

There are times when you need an easy noodle recipe, and this one fits the bill. If you don't want to turn on the stove, you can also eat them raw. These noodles are wonderful with Slow Cooker Spaghetti Sauce (page 50), Pesto (page 48), or Thai Almond Sauce (page 52).

PREP TIME
5 min

COOK TIME
1 min

MAKES
2 servings

INGREDIENTS

1 large zucchini

4 cups water

DIET

AIP

1. Cut the ends off the zucchini and spiral-slice it on the small noodle setting. Slice the noodles in half crosswise.

2. Bring the water to a boil in a large saucepan. Drop the noodles into the boiling water and cook for 1 minute.

3. Drain and serve immediately.

Sweet Potato Fries

No joke, I can eat my weight in these sweet potato fries. They're best when you let them cook until they are a dark golden color—not burnt, mind you, but so they have a little crunch. You can serve these fries with almost all of the condiments in this book: Homemade Mayo (page 30), Ranch Dressing (page 38), Honey Mustard (page 40), Hot Sauce (page 46), and, of course, Ketchup (page 28).

PREP TIME   COOK TIME   MAKES

10 min   20 min   4 servings

INGREDIENTS

4 cups lard

2 tablespoons tapioca flour

½ teaspoon sea salt

2 large sweet potatoes (about 3 pounds), cut into ½-by-3-inch sticks

DIET   OCCASION

 AIP

Game day

1. In a 9-inch cast-iron skillet, heat the lard to 375°F. Preheat the oven to 200°F. Line a rimmed baking sheet with a paper towel.

2. Mix the tapioca flour and salt in a large bowl. Add the sweet potato sticks and toss to coat.

3. Fry half of the potatoes, stirring occasionally, until golden brown and crispy, 6 to 8 minutes. Remove from the pan with a slotted spoon and place on the prepared baking sheet, spreading them out so they don't overlap. Place in the oven to keep warm while you fry the rest of the potatoes. Serve hot.

CHAPTER 6

DESSERTS

Chocolate Chip Cookies

I want to change the saying "It's as American as apple pie" to "It's as American as chocolate chip cookies." This classic cookie is well loved, and for good reason: it's a sweet little gem of chocolate-studded goodness. In this recipe, the dates give it a rich, buttery flavor that can't be beat and an added warmth that will remind you of your grandmother's recipe. These are addictive. I love eating them with a big glass of cold coconut milk.

PREP TIME   COOK TIME   MAKES

10 min   12 min   18 cookies

INGREDIENTS

8 whole Deglet Noor dates, pitted

2 cups blanched, superfine almond flour

½ cup unsweetened shredded coconut

1 large egg

1 tablespoon maple syrup

½ teaspoon vanilla extract

¼ teaspoon ground cinnamon

¼ teaspoon sea salt

½ cup dark chocolate chips

1. Preheat the oven to 350°F. Line two baking sheets with parchment paper.

2. Place the dates in a food processor and pulse for 30 seconds to break them up. Add the almond flour, coconut, egg, maple syrup, vanilla extract, cinnamon, and salt and pulse for 1 minute to combine.

3. With a spoon, mix in the chocolate chips.

4. Shape a large spoonful of dough into a 2-inch ball and place on a prepared baking sheet. With a cup, flatten the ball to ½ inch thick. Repeat with the rest of the dough, placing the cookies about an inch apart.

5. Bake for 10 to 12 minutes, until golden brown, switching the positions of the baking sheets halfway through. Remove from the oven and let cool on a rack before serving.

6. Store leftovers in an airtight container at room temperature for 3 to 5 days.

Carrot Cake

What's not to like about a rich, moist cake filled with spices, grated carrots, and raisins? The first time I had carrot cake, I was six years old and had no idea what it was—I had only had yellow and chocolate cake—but after my first bite, I was in love. So was my brother, who was later found in the kitchen finishing off the leftover cake. Not surprisingly, he had a stomachache that night. But as long as you don't eat it all in one sitting, this all-star cake is perfect for any special occasion.

PREP TIME 25 min

COOK TIME 30 min

MAKES
1
2-layer,
9-inch cake

INGREDIENTS

1 cup melted coconut oil, plus more for greasing the pans

10 large eggs, at room temperature

2 teaspoons vanilla extract

¼ cup honey

2 cups unsweetened applesauce

1 cup coconut flour

1½ tablespoons pumpkin pie spice

1 teaspoon baking powder

1 teaspoon baking soda

3 medium carrots, peeled and finely grated

½ cup raisins (optional)

1 batch Vanilla Frosting (page 220)

OCCASION

Birthday

1. Preheat the oven to 350°F. Grease two 9-inch round cake pans.

2. In a large bowl, mix together the melted coconut oil, eggs, vanilla extract, honey, and applesauce with a handheld electric mixer until completely blended.

3. Add the coconut flour, pumpkin pie spice, baking powder, and baking soda and mix with a spatula until fully blended.

4. Fold in the grated carrots and raisins, if using.

5. Divide the batter evenly between the two prepared cake pans. Bake for 30 minutes, or until a toothpick inserted in the center comes out clean.

6. Remove from the oven and let cool in the pans.

7. To release the cakes, run a knife around the outer edge. Place a serving platter on top of one of the pans and flip the cake onto the platter. Spread one-quarter of the frosting over the top of the cake.

8. Carefully remove the second layer from the pan in the same way and gently place it on top of the first layer. Use the remaining frosting to cover the top and sides.

9. Cut into slices and serve. Any leftovers will keep for 3 to 4 days in the fridge.

Vanilla Frosting

Yes, I was that kid who ate frosting right out of the tub. I mostly grew out of it, but it's hard to resist this fluffy, sweet frosting. If you want to mix it up, you can swap out the vanilla for other flavor extracts, like almond, orange, and peppermint.

PREP TIME
5 min

MAKES
1¼ cups

INGREDIENTS

1 cup palm shortening, solid but not chilled (see Note)

¼ cup maple syrup

2 teaspoons vanilla extract

½ teaspoon lemon juice

1. Place the palm shortening in a small bowl and whip with a handheld electric mixer for 1 minute, until smooth.

2. Add the maple syrup, vanilla extract, and lemon juice and blend on medium speed for 2 minutes, until fluffy.

NOTE: Palm shortening is nearly impossible to work with when it's chilled, so make sure it's both solid and at room temperature. If you live in a hot climate or make this frosting during the summer, your palm shortening may liquefy at room temperature. If that happens, chill it until it becomes solid and then let it warm (but not melt) before making the frosting.

"Oatmeal" Raisin Cookies

In my pre-Paleo days, I was a die-hard oatmeal raisin cookie fan, and now this cookie helps me get my fix. Raisins, cinnamon, and unsweetened shredded coconut turn this simple recipe into "oatmeal" raisin cookie magic. The cookies bake up lightly crispy on the outside but stay perfectly soft on the inside. You can easily add chocolate chips or dates to make it your own.

PREP TIME
10 min

COOK TIME
20 min

MAKES
12 cookies

INGREDIENTS

1 cup smooth almond butter

1 large egg

½ teaspoon vanilla extract

¼ cup plus 1 tablespoon maple syrup

½ cup raisins

½ cup unsweetened shredded coconut

½ teaspoon sea salt

½ teaspoon baking soda

½ teaspoon ground cinnamon

1. Preheat the oven to 350°F. Line a baking sheet with parchment paper or a silicone baking mat.

2. In a large mixing bowl, combine the almond butter, egg, vanilla extract, and maple syrup and beat with a wooden spoon for 1 minute, until smooth.

3. Add the raisins, coconut, salt, baking soda, and cinnamon and mix for 1 minute, until thoroughly combined.

4. Drop the dough by the tablespoonful onto the prepared baking sheet. Leave at least 2 inches between the cookies, as they will spread.

5. Bake for 18 to 20 minutes, until light golden brown.

6. Remove from the oven and let cool on a rack before serving. Store leftovers in an airtight jar at room temperature for 4 to 5 days.

No-Bake Chocolate Raspberry "Cheesecake"

I know what you're thinking. Yes, there are a lot of steps to this recipe, but it is so worth it. The flavor of the raspberries and chocolate over the almond crust is heavenly. The avocado may be unexpected, but it adds a creamy richness, and I promise you that it will be the last thing on your mind after you take your first bite. Instead of chilling the cake in the fridge, you can place it in the freezer for 3 hours for a firmer texture, similar to that of an ice cream cake.

PREP TIME

30 min

plus 6 hours to chill

MAKES

1

1-layer, 9-inch cake

INGREDIENTS

coconut oil, for greasing the pan

Crust

2 cups unsalted roasted almonds

¼ teaspoon sea salt

2 tablespoons coconut oil

½ teaspoon ground cinnamon

15 whole Deglet Noor dates, pitted

Coconut mixture

½ cup melted coconut oil

1 cup canned, full-fat coconut milk

2 tablespoons beef gelatin

2 teaspoons vanilla extract

½ teaspoon sea salt

Raspberry layer

1 (2-ounce) bag freeze-dried raspberries

3 large ripe bananas, halved

1 large avocado, halved, pitted, and peeled

half of coconut mixture (from above)

Chocolate layer

6 whole Deglet Noor dates, pitted

2 large avocados, halved, pitted, and peeled

1 large ripe banana, chopped

3 tablespoons honey

¼ cup unsweetened cacao powder

remaining half of coconut mixture (from above)

1. Line the bottom of a 9-inch springform pan with a large sheet of parchment paper, allowing the paper to overhang and extend beyond the rim of the pan. Grease the sides of the pan.

2. Make the crust: Place the almonds in a food processor and pulse for 30 seconds, until you have a coarse crumble.

3. Add the salt, coconut oil, and cinnamon and turn on the food processor. Drop the dates one by one into the mixture until fully combined.

4. Press this mixture evenly across the bottom of the prepared springform pan. Set aside. Thoroughly clean and dry the food processor.

5. Make the coconut mixture: In a large saucepan over medium heat, place the melted coconut oil, coconut milk, gelatin, vanilla extract, and salt and whisk to combine. Cook for 3 minutes, then remove the pan from the heat and set aside.

6. Make the raspberry layer: Place the freeze-dried raspberries in the clean food processor and pulse until you have a fine powder. Add the bananas, avocado, and half of the coconut mixture. Pulse until smooth. Pour this mixture over the almond crust to form the raspberry layer. Thoroughly clean and dry the food processor.

7. Make the chocolate layer: Place the dates in the clean food processor and pulse for 30 seconds. Add the avocados, banana, honey, cacao powder, and the rest of the coconut mixture. Pulse until smooth, then drop by large spoonfuls over the raspberry layer, and gently spread it evenly all over the surface.

8. Place in the refrigerator to chill for 6 hours.

9. To remove the cake from the springform pan, run a knife around the edge and carefully remove the sides of the pan. Using the parchment paper, slide the cake off the base.

10. Cut into slices and serve. You can store this cake in the fridge for 3 to 4 days or freeze it and defrost as needed.

NOTE: If you have an immersion blender, you can use it to make the raspberry and chocolate layers, saving you from cleaning your food processor repeatedly.

OCCASION

Birthday

Valentine's Day

Peach Cobbler

Peach cobbler reminds me of my Southern roots, and it's one of my father's favorites. At a family get-together in Louisiana, a line of people were fighting over my grandmother's peach cobbler. I snuck a bite from my father's plate, and it was sugary-sweet peachy heaven. This recipe is an homage to that dish. Warm, soft peaches, lightly sweetened and topped with a crust that is easy to make and even easier to eat: it's hard to resist.

PREP TIME
20 min

COOK TIME
1 hour

MAKES
8 servings

INGREDIENTS

2 pounds frozen sliced peaches

¼ cup tapioca flour

¼ teaspoon sea salt

½ teaspoon ground cinnamon

¼ teaspoon ground nutmeg

¼ cup maple syrup

2 tablespoons lemon juice

Crust

2 cups blanched, superfine almond flour

½ teaspoon baking soda

¼ teaspoon ground nutmeg

¼ cup palm shortening

1 large egg, beaten

1 tablespoon maple syrup

1. Preheat the oven to 350°F.

2. Place the peaches in an 8-inch square baking dish. Sprinkle them with the tapioca flour, salt, cinnamon, and nutmeg, then drizzle the maple syrup and lemon juice over the top. Mix with a spoon until the peaches are well coated.

3. Make the crust: In a medium bowl, combine the almond flour, baking soda, nutmeg, and palm shortening and mix with a fork until you have a crumbly mixture. Add the egg and maple syrup and stir until a dough forms.

4. Place the dough between two sheets of parchment paper and roll it out to an 8-inch square that is ½ inch thick.

5. Place the rolled-out crust over the peach mixture. Bake for 1 hour, or until golden brown.

6. Remove from the oven and let cool until no longer hot but still warm, and serve.

Grasshopper Pudding

Silky, rich peppermint pudding topped with chocolate cookie crumbles: I don't know about you, but that sounds a lot like a love song to me. This recipe is lightning-fast to make and will disappear just as quickly. You can turn this pudding into a completely different treat by omitting the peppermint oil and adding berries, toasted nuts, or dark chocolate chips.

PREP TIME

12 min

MAKES
2
servings

INGREDIENTS

Peppermint pudding

1 large ripe avocado, halved, pitted, and peeled

2 large ripe bananas, chopped

½ cup melted coconut oil

½ teaspoon peppermint oil

¼ teaspoon sea salt

Chocolate cookie crumble

1 cup blanched, superfine almond flour

3 tablespoons cacao powder

2 tablespoons honey

1 tablespoon melted coconut oil

1. Make the pudding: In a food processor, combine the avocado, bananas, coconut oil, peppermint oil, and salt and process until smooth, roughly 1 minute.

2. Make the chocolate cookie crumble: In a medium bowl, combine the almond flour, cacao powder, honey, and coconut oil and mix with a spoon until you have a rough crumble, about 30 seconds.

3. In each of two medium glasses, place ½ cup of the chocolate cookie crumble, then add half of the pudding mixture. Top each glass with half of the remaining chocolate cookie crumble. Serve immediately.

Almond Butter Sandwich Cookies

These soft almond butter cookies are doubly good with a velvety chocolate cream filling sandwiched between them. I liken them to a double-decker bus of cookie happiness, and they make the perfect after-school treat. You can also put them in the freezer for a nutty frozen treat.

PREP TIME
20 min

plus 20 min to chill

COOK TIME
18 min

MAKES
10 cookies

INGREDIENTS

Cookies

1 cup smooth almond butter

¼ cup coconut flour

2 large eggs, beaten

½ teaspoon sea salt

½ teaspoon baking soda

3 tablespoons maple syrup

1 teaspoon vanilla extract

¼ cup palm shortening

Chocolate cream filling

¼ cup palm shortening

¼ cup smooth almond butter

2 tablespoons maple syrup

½ teaspoon vanilla extract

1 tablespoon cacao powder

1. Preheat the oven to 350°F. Line two baking sheets with parchment paper or silicone baking mats.

2. Make the cookies: In a large mixing bowl, combine the almond butter, coconut flour, eggs, salt, baking soda, maple syrup, vanilla extract, and palm shortening. Mix with a wooden spoon until smooth.

3. Shape the dough into 2-inch balls and place them 1 inch apart on the prepared baking sheets. Press with a fork to ½ inch thick, then turn the fork and press again lightly to make a crosshatch pattern.

4. Bake for 15 to 18 minutes, until light golden brown, switching the positions of the baking sheets halfway through. Remove from the oven and let cool on the baking sheets.

5. Make the chocolate cream filling: In a small bowl, combine the palm shortening, almond butter, maple syrup, vanilla extract, and cacao powder. With a handheld electric mixer, blend on medium speed for 1 minute, until smooth.

6. Spread the filling on the flat side of half of the cooled cookies and top with the remaining cookies to create sandwiches. Refrigerate for 20 minutes to allow the filling to stiffen slightly.

Banana Cream Pie

Don't wait for a special occasion to whip up this dreamy mixture of bananas and coconut cream. The billowy whipped cream topping makes each bite more delectable than the last. If you have a weakness for banana cream pie, as I do, then this version needs to be on your table, stat.

PREP TIME

15 min

plus 25 min for the pie crust and 2 hours to chill

MAKES

1

(8-inch) pie

INGREDIENTS

1 Basic Pie Crust (page 82), prebaked and cooled

4 large ripe bananas, divided

2 tablespoons lemon juice

1 cup melted coconut oil, slightly warm

½ teaspoon vanilla extract

¼ teaspoon sea salt

¼ teaspoon ground cinnamon

1 tablespoon beef gelatin

3 tablespoons maple syrup

1 batch Whipped Coconut Cream (page 234)

1. Have a prebaked 8-inch pie shell ready to fill.

2. Slice three of the bananas and lightly toss them with the lemon juice to coat. Place in the prebaked pie shell.

3. In a blender, combine the remaining banana, coconut oil, vanilla extract, salt, cinnamon, gelatin, and maple syrup. Blend for 1 minute, until smooth, and then pour over the sliced bananas.

4. Place the pie in the refrigerator and let chill for 2 hours. Remove from the refrigerator, top with the whipped cream, and serve.

NOTE: You can make this recipe AIP-compliant by using the dough from Cherry Toaster Pastries (page 68). Prepare the dough, press it into an 8-inch pie pan, and bake for 10 minutes, or until light golden brown.

Whipped Coconut Cream

This simple, dairy-free whipped topping is perfect for cream pies and is a great way to dress up a bowl of fruit. For this recipe to come out perfectly, you must chill the canned coconut milk overnight.

PREP TIME

5 min

MAKES

1 cup

plus 12 hours to chill the coconut milk

INGREDIENTS

1 (13½-ounce) can full-fat coconut milk, chilled overnight (see Note)

½ teaspoon vanilla extract

1 teaspoon tapioca flour

1 tablespoon maple syrup

1. Open the can of coconut milk and gently remove the solid coconut cream that has risen to the top. (Save the leftover coconut water to use in smoothies.)

2. Place the coconut cream in a large bowl and whip with a handheld electric mixer or an immersion blender for 1 to 2 minutes, until soft peaks form.

3. Add the vanilla extract, tapioca flour, and maple syrup. Whip for 30 seconds, until the ingredients are combined and the texture is smooth and fluffy.

4. This cream will keep in a sealed container in the fridge for 3 to 4 days.

NOTE: The best brands of coconut milk to use for making whipped coconut cream are Thai Kitchen Organic and Natural Value Organic.

Key Lime Pie

I had a tough time finding Key limes, so I used readily available regular limes (called Persian limes) to make this tasty dessert. I know, I know, I should be ashamed of myself, but honestly, when I started eating, all I felt was the overwhelming urge to eat another bite. This semi-tart pie is everything it should be, whether you use regular lime juice or Key lime juice.

PREP TIME

15 min

MAKES
1
(8-inch) pie

plus 25 min for the pie crust and 2 hours to chill

INGREDIENTS

1 Basic Pie Crust (page 82), prebaked and cooled

½ cup Key lime juice or regular lime juice

1½ tablespoons beef gelatin

1 cup melted coconut oil, slightly warm

3 large ripe bananas

3 tablespoons maple syrup

grated zest of 1 lime

1 batch Whipped Coconut Cream (page 234)

lime slices, for garnish (optional)

1. Have a prebaked 8-inch pie shell ready to fill.

2. In a blender, combine the lime juice and gelatin and pulse for 10 seconds. Add the melted coconut oil, bananas, maple syrup, and lime zest and pulse until smooth.

3. Pour into the prebaked pie shell and place in the refrigerator for 2 hours.

4. Remove the pie from the refrigerator and top with the whipped coconut cream. Garnish with lime slices, if desired.

NOTE: You can make this recipe AIP-compliant by using the dough from Cherry Toaster Pastries (page 68). Prepare the dough, press it into an 8-inch pie pan, and bake for 10 minutes, or until light golden brown.

Devil's Food Cake

This cake is so decadent, it's for adults only. It is lightly sweet, with a heady flavor of rich dark chocolate that will have you asking for thirds. It's best served at room temperature, but it's still an amazing indulgence right out of the fridge.

PREP TIME

35 min

COOK TIME

20 min

MAKES
1
2-layer,
6-inch cake

INGREDIENTS

1 cup melted coconut oil, plus more for greasing the pans

1 cup blanched, superfine almond flour

½ cup coconut flour

1 teaspoon baking soda

½ teaspoon sea salt

5 large eggs, at room temperature

4 ounces unsweetened baking chocolate, melted

½ cup unsweetened applesauce, at room temperature

¼ cup maple syrup

1 teaspoon vanilla extract

Chocolate frosting

1 cup palm shortening, solid but not chilled

3 tablespoons cacao powder

3 tablespoons maple syrup

1 teaspoon vanilla extract

¼ teaspoon sea salt

OCCASION

Birthday

1. Preheat the oven to 350°F. Grease two 6-inch round cake pans.

2. In a large bowl, combine the almond flour, coconut flour, baking soda, and salt and mix well.

3. In a separate bowl, combine the eggs, melted coconut oil, melted chocolate, applesauce, maple syrup, and vanilla extract and blend with a whisk.

4. Add the wet ingredients to the dry ingredients and whisk until smooth.

5. Pour the batter evenly into the prepared pans. Bake for 20 minutes, or until a toothpick inserted in the center comes out either clean or with only a few crumbs clinging to it. Remove from the oven and let cool completely in the pans.

6. While the cakes are cooling, make the frosting: Place the palm shortening in a small bowl and whip it with a handheld electric mixer for 1 minute, until smooth and fluffy.

7. Add the cacao powder, maple syrup, vanilla extract, and salt and blend on medium speed for 2 minutes, until smooth.

8. To release the cakes from the pans, run a knife around their outer edges. Place a serving platter on top of one of the pans and flip the cake onto the platter. Spread one-quarter of the frosting over the top of the cake.

9. Carefully remove the second layer from the pan in the same way and gently place it on top of the first layer. Spread the remaining frosting over the top and sides.

10. Cut into slices and serve. This cake will keep for 3 to 4 days in the fridge.

NOTE: Palm shortening is nearly impossible to work with when it's chilled, so make sure it's both solid and at room temperature. If you live in a hot climate or make this frosting during the summer, your palm shortening may liquefy at room temperature. If that happens, chill it until it becomes solid and then let it warm (but not melt) before making the frosting.

Chocolate-Covered Strawberries

Making homemade chocolate-covered strawberries is a breeze, and the addition of salt, cinnamon, and cayenne in the coating makes for a fun surprise. This recipe is great way to get your kids involved in the kitchen, and they will have a sweet treat to enjoy when they're done.

PREP TIME   COOK TIME   MAKES
10 min   10 min   8 servings

INGREDIENTS

Chocolate coating

4 ounces unsweetened baking chocolate

3 tablespoons maple syrup

¼ teaspoon sea salt

¼ teaspoon ground cinnamon

¼ teaspoon cayenne pepper

1 pound strawberries with stems, washed and dried very well

OCCASION

Valentine's Day

1. Line a baking sheet with parchment paper.

2. In a double boiler over medium heat, melt the chocolate.

3. Add the maple syrup, salt, cinnamon, and cayenne pepper and whisk until smooth.

4. Dip the strawberries into the coating and set them on the prepared baking sheet until the chocolate has hardened.

5. These will keep in the refrigerator for 1 week.

NOTE: If fresh strawberries aren't available, you can use in-season fruit like pears or oranges instead.

Apple Pie Ice Cream

I scream, you scream, we all scream for apple pie ice cream. This recipe is a fun twist on the classic baked pie and makes the perfect sweet treat for hot summer days. You can top it with Granola (page 110) to kick it up a notch.

PREP TIME	COOK TIME	MAKES
30 min	8 min	3½ cups

INGREDIENTS

Apple filling

1 medium tart apple such as Granny Smith, peeled, cored, and diced

3 tablespoons water

2 tablespoons coconut oil or ghee

1 tablespoon maple syrup

1 teaspoon pumpkin pie spice

¼ teaspoon sea salt

Ice cream

2 (13½-ounce) cans full-fat coconut milk

¼ cup maple syrup

1 teaspoon vanilla extract

½ teaspoon pumpkin pie spice

¼ teaspoon sea salt

1. Make the filling: In a saucepan over low heat, combine the diced apple, water, coconut oil, maple syrup, pumpkin pie spice, and salt. Cook until the water has evaporated and the apples are soft but not mushy, about 8 minutes. Remove from the heat and set aside.

2. Make the ice cream: In a blender, combine the coconut milk, maple syrup, vanilla extract, pumpkin pie spice, and salt. Blend until well mixed, roughly 1 minute.

3. Fold the apple filling into the ice cream with a spoon. Pour the liquid into your ice cream maker and churn for 20 minutes or until firm. If it's still soft, you can place it in the freezer for 2 hours to harden.

NOTE: You can make this recipe AIP-compliant by using ground cinnamon in place of the pumpkin pie spice.

Apple Pie

Coconut sugar gives this apple pie a rich caramel flavor that can't be beat. It took me a while to figure out how to get the apples perfectly soft but not mushy, so that even my mushy texture–adverse husband would approve. Pre-cooking the apples does the trick!

PREP TIME   COOK TIME   MAKES

 15 min    45 min   1 (8-inch) pie

plus 15 min for the pie crusts

INGREDIENTS

2 batches Basic Pie Crust dough (page 82), unbaked

Filling

3 pounds Granny Smith apples, peeled, cored, and sliced

3 tablespoons tapioca flour

2 tablespoons water

1 teaspoon vanilla extract

1 teaspoon pumpkin pie spice

½ teaspoon sea salt

½ cup coconut sugar

1. Line the bottom of an 8-inch pie pan with one pie crust and set the other aside.

2. Make the filling: In a large pot over medium heat, combine the apples, tapioca flour, water, vanilla extract, pumpkin pie spice, salt, and sugar and stir to evenly coat the apple slices. Cover and cook for 20 minutes, stirring occasionally. The apple slices should be soft but not mushy. Remove from the heat and let cool.

3. While the filling is cooling, preheat the oven to 350°F.

4. Pour the cooled apple filling into the pie shell and cover with the second crust. Trim off any overhang and crimp the edges to seal.

5. Bake for 25 minutes, or until golden brown. Remove from the oven and let cool completely before serving.

Cream-Filled Chocolate Cupcakes

When I think of how many cream-filled chocolate cupcakes I've eaten without wondering how the filling got inside them, I'm rather embarrassed. It's actually easier than you'd think to make the secret compartment in these cupcakes, and the extra effort was worth it when I saw the look of puzzlement and then sheer happiness on my son's face after he took his first bite.

PREP TIME **25** min

COOK TIME **20** min

MAKES **12** cupcakes

plus 5 min for the whipped cream and 1 hour to chill

INGREDIENTS

coconut oil, for greasing the pan

2 cups blanched, superfine almond flour

1 teaspoon baking soda

½ teaspoon salt

2 ounces unsweetened baking chocolate, melted

2 large eggs, at room temperature

½ cup water

½ cup melted coconut oil

¼ cup maple syrup

Chocolate frosting

1 cup palm shortening, solid but not chilled

3 tablespoons cacao powder

3 tablespoons maple syrup

1 teaspoon vanilla extract

¼ teaspoon sea salt

1 batch Whipped Coconut Cream (page 234)

OCCASION

Birthday

1. Preheat the oven to 350°F. Grease a 12-cup muffin tin.

2. In a mixing bowl, combine the almond flour, baking soda, and salt and mix with a spoon.

3. Add the melted chocolate, eggs, water, melted coconut oil, and maple syrup and mix until smooth.

4. Pour the batter evenly into the cups of the prepared muffin tin, filling each cup about three-quarters full. Bake for 15 to 20 minutes, until a toothpick inserted into the center of a cupcake comes out clean.

5. Remove from the oven and let cool in the pan.

6. While the cupcakes are cooling, make the frosting: Place the palm shortening in a small bowl and whip it with a handheld electric mixer for 1 minute, until smooth and fluffy.

7. Add the cacao powder, maple syrup, vanilla extract, and salt and blend on medium speed for 2 minutes, until smooth.

8. To fill the cupcakes, cut a 1-inch-deep hole on the bottom of each cupcake and save a piece to use as a cap. Set aside ¼ cup of the whipped coconut cream and use the rest to fill the holes. Close the holes with the caps.

9. Frost the top of each cupcake with the chocolate frosting. Fill a piping bag with the reserved ¼ cup of whipped coconut cream. Pipe decorative curls across the top of each cupcake.

10. Chill in the refrigerator for 1 hour before serving to allow the filling to stiffen slightly. These cupcakes will keep for 3 to 4 days stored in a sealed container in the fridge.

Chocolate Sandwich Cookies

I dare you to eat just one of these cookies! They are delicate little chocolate sandwich bites that also freeze into the perfect "ice cream" cookies. I never understood why anyone would just eat the filling and miss out on the chocolate cookies until I made these with homemade vanilla frosting. Now I make them with double-thick centers because the filling tastes so good!

PREP TIME   20 min

plus 20 min to chill

COOK TIME   18 min

MAKES 8 cookies

INGREDIENTS

Cookies

1 cup blanched, superfine almond flour

¼ cup coconut flour

2 tablespoons cacao powder

½ teaspoon sea salt

3 tablespoons maple syrup

1 large egg

Filling

1 batch Vanilla Frosting (page 220)

1. Preheat the oven to 350°F. Line a baking sheet with parchment paper or a silicone baking mat.

2. Make the cookies: In a small bowl, combine the almond flour, coconut flour, cacao powder, and salt and stir to combine.

3. Add the maple syrup and egg and mix until you have a soft dough.

4. Roll out the dough between two sheets of parchment paper until it is ¼ inch thick. With a cookie cutter, cut out 16 circles 2 inches in diameter. Place the dough circles on the prepared baking sheet, spaced 1 inch apart.

5. Bake for 15 to 18 minutes, until firmly set. Remove from the oven and let cool completely on the baking sheet.

6. Assemble the cookies: Spread the frosting on the flat side of half of the cookies. Top each frosted cookie with a second cookie to create a total of eight sandwiches.

7. Refrigerate for 20 minutes before serving to allow the filling to stiffen slightly. Store these cookies at room temperature in an airtight container for 3 to 4 days.

Creamy Hazelnut and Chocolate Pie

My mother-in-law's killer peanut butter cream pie was the inspiration for this recipe. Pairing home-roasted hazelnuts with a dark chocolate topping creates an unforgettable flavor. This pie will disappear before your eyes!

PREP TIME

20 min

COOK TIME
12 min

MAKES
1 (8-inch) pie

plus 25 min for the pie crust and 1½ hours to chill

INGREDIENTS

1 Basic Pie Crust (page 82), prebaked and cooled

Filling

1 cup raw hazelnuts

1 cup unsweetened applesauce

½ cup melted coconut oil, slightly warm

3 tablespoons maple syrup

½ teaspoon vanilla extract

¼ teaspoon sea salt

1 tablespoon beef gelatin

Chocolate topping

2 tablespoons cacao powder

2 tablespoons maple syrup

2 tablespoons melted coconut oil

1. Have a prebaked pie shell ready to fill.

2. Preheat the oven to 350°F.

3. Roast the hazelnuts: Place the hazelnuts in a single layer on a rimmed baking sheet and bake for 8 to 12 minutes. Check them every 5 minutes and shake the pan so they roast evenly. When perfectly roasted, the skins will be blistered and the nuts will be very fragrant. Remove from the oven and transfer to a plate to cool completely.

4. Wrap the hazelnuts in a clean dish towel and massage them. Most of the skins will flake off.

5. Make the filling: Place the roasted, skinned hazelnuts in a food processor and grind into a nut butter, roughly 2 minutes, stopping the machine once or twice to scrape down the sides.

6. Add the applesauce and coconut oil and pulse for 30 seconds, until you have a puree. Then add the vanilla extract, maple syrup, salt, and gelatin and pulse for 30 seconds.

7. Pour the nut mixture into the prebaked pie shell and chill for 1 hour.

8. Make the chocolate topping: In a small bowl, whisk together the cacao powder, maple syrup, and melted coconut oil until smooth. Pour this mixture evenly over the top of the pie and spread with a rubber spatula.

9. Return the pie to the fridge and chill for an additional 30 minutes before slicing and serving.

Unfried Ice Cream

My surprisingly simple version takes classic fried ice cream to a whole new level of deliciousness. I didn't want to spend hours coating, freezing, and then frying the ice cream before I could get it into my belly, so I came up with this ground coconut coating that creates a texture that's close to the batter used in the real deal, with no need for frying.

PREP TIME	COOK TIME	MAKES
35 min	5 min	7–8 scoops

plus 2 hours to chill

INGREDIENTS

Vanilla ice cream

1 (13½-ounce) can full-fat coconut milk

1 teaspoon vanilla extract

2 tablespoons honey

2 tablespoons tapioca flour

Crumb coating

⅓ cup unsweetened coconut flakes (see Note)

⅓ cup blanched, superfine almond flour

1 teaspoon ground cinnamon

1 batch Whipped Coconut Cream (page 234), for serving (optional)

fresh berries of choice, for serving (optional)

1. Make the ice cream: In a saucepan over medium-high heat, whisk together the coconut milk, vanilla extract, honey, and tapioca flour. Bring just to a boil and remove from the heat immediately. Pour into a heatproof bowl and set in the refrigerator for 1 hour to chill.

2. Pour the chilled ice cream base into your ice cream maker and churn, following the manufacturer's directions, for 20 minutes, or until set.

3. Line a half-size rimmed baking sheet with parchment paper. With an ice cream scoop, scoop a ball of ice cream and place it on the lined baking sheet. Repeat with the remaining ice cream. (This recipe makes seven or eight balls.) Set the ice cream balls in the freezer for 1 hour to firm up.

4. Make the coating: Place the coconut flakes in a food processor and pulse for 20 seconds, until you have large shreds.

5. Transfer the coconut to a large bowl. Add the almond flour and cinnamon and mix with a spoon.

6. Remove the ice cream balls from the freezer and let sit for 1 minute to soften slightly. Roll each ice cream ball in the crumb coating until thickly coated.

7. Top with whipped coconut cream and/or fresh berries, if desired, and serve immediately.

NOTE: You can use unsweetened shredded coconut instead of coconut flakes if you prefer. Just reduce the amount to ¼ cup and skip the step of grinding it in the food processor. But keep in mind that the ground flakes create a crumb-like texture that's closer to the fried batter of the classic dish.

Pecan Pie

I cannot remember a single holiday when I did not have pecan pie. My mother made four of these pies every Thanksgiving and Christmas, and I'm sure that if she hadn't, we all would have had a four-alarm temper tantrum. This recipe has the perfect amount of sweetness, and you would never know that it's grain-free!

PREP TIME

15 min

plus 10 min for the pie crust

COOK TIME
30 min

MAKES
1
(8-inch) pie

INGREDIENTS

1 batch Basic Pie Crust dough (page 82), unbaked

2 cups roasted, unsalted pecan halves

4 large eggs

½ cup honey

2 tablespoons melted coconut oil

1 teaspoon vanilla extract

½ teaspoon pumpkin pie spice

OCCASION

Holiday

1. Preheat the oven to 350°F.

2. Line an 8-inch pie pan with the pie crust. Place the pecans in the pie shell and set aside.

3. In a large bowl, combine the eggs, honey, melted coconut oil, vanilla extract, and pumpkin pie spice and whisk until smooth. Pour this mixture over the pecans.

4. Bake for 25 to 30 minutes, until the edges of the filling are set but the center is still slightly loose.

5. Remove from the oven and let cool completely before serving.

Pumpkin Pie

I never really understood the appeal of pumpkin pie until I made one with fresh roasted pumpkin instead of canned. Holy smokes, it was like going from black-and-white TV to 1080p HD. (Of course, if you're making this pie when fresh pumpkins aren't in season, you can use canned pumpkin puree instead.) In addition to fresh roasted pumpkin, this recipe has another delicious twist that makes it really special: apple butter.

PREP TIME   COOK TIME   MAKES

10 min   45 min   1 (8-inch) pie

plus 2½ hours to roast the pumpkins and 10 min for the pie crust

INGREDIENTS

1 batch Basic Pie Crust dough (page 82), unbaked

2 scant cups puréed, fresh-roasted pie pumpkin or 1 (15-ounce) can pumpkin puree

¼ cup apple butter

¼ cup honey

½ cup canned, full-fat coconut milk

1 teaspoon pumpkin pie spice

1 teaspoon vanilla extract

¼ teaspoon sea salt

2 large eggs

1 batch Whipped Coconut Cream (page 234), for serving (optional)

OCCASION

Holiday

1. Preheat the oven to 350°F.

2. Line an 8-inch pie pan with the pie crust and set aside.

3. In a blender, combine the pumpkin puree, apple butter, honey, coconut milk, pumpkin pie spice, vanilla extract, salt, and eggs and blend for 3 minutes or until completely mixed.

4. Pour the pumpkin mixture into the pie shell. Bake for 40 to 45 minutes, until a toothpick inserted 1 inch from the crust comes out clean.

5. Remove from the oven and let cool completely before serving. Serve topped with whipped coconut cream, if desired.

HOW TO MAKE FRESH ROASTED PUMPKIN PUREE

INGREDIENTS
Pie pumpkins (for this recipe, about 2 pounds)

TOOLS
Sharp knife, rimmed baking sheet, food processor

1. Preheat the oven to 350°F. Slice the pumpkins in half and scoop out the seeds with a spoon, working from bottom to top to go with the grain.

2. Place the pumpkins cut side up on a rimmed baking sheet. Bake until the flesh is very tender and the skin is shriveled, about 2 hours. Scoop the cooked pumpkin flesh into a food processor and process for 2 minutes, until completely smooth.

3. The pumpkin puree will keep for 1 week in an airtight container in the fridge, or you can freeze it in freezer-safe wide-mouth jars and defrost as needed.

Kitchen Sink Cookies

Have you ever wanted to whip up a batch of chocolate chip cookies and found that you just didn't have enough chocolate chips? It's times like those that I start rummaging through my pantry to see what else I can find, and voilà, the Kitchen Sink Cookie was born. You can throw in whatever sweet morsels you have in your pantry to make it your own.

PREP TIME   COOK TIME   MAKES

10 min   15 min   18 cookies

INGREDIENTS

15 whole Deglet Noor dates, pitted

2 cups blanched, superfine almond flour

½ teaspoon sea salt

½ teaspoon baking soda

½ teaspoon ground cinnamon

1 teaspoon vanilla extract

1 large egg

½ cup unsweetened shredded coconut

¼ cup dark chocolate chips

¼ cup raisins

1 tablespoon raw sesame seeds

1. Preheat the oven to 350°F. Line two baking sheets with parchment paper or silicone baking mats.

2. In a food processor, pulse the dates until minced, roughly 30 seconds. Add the almond flour, salt, baking soda, and cinnamon and pulse for 30 seconds. Add the vanilla extract and egg and pulse until you have a slightly stiff dough.

3. Using a spoon, mix in the shredded coconut, chocolate chips, raisins, and sesame seeds until well combined.

4. Roll the dough into 2-inch balls and set on the prepared baking sheets 1 inch apart. With a cup, press the balls to ½ inch thick.

5. Bake for 12 to 15 minutes, until firmly set, switching the positions of the baking sheets halfway through.

6. Remove from the oven and let cool on a rack before serving. Store these cookies in an airtight container at room temperature for 3 to 4 days.

CHAPTER 7

DRINKS

Salted Chocolate Smoothie

Sweet and salty chocolate goodness, this smoothie is like heaven on a hot day. I love sneaking gelatin into my smoothies because it's an amazing superfood. When I remember, I also add some green powder. My son asks for this smoothie every single day.

PREP TIME

5 min

MAKES
2
servings

INGREDIENTS

2 large ripe bananas

1 cup ice cubes

2 cups Coconut Milk (page 34)

3 tablespoons cacao powder

½ teaspoon sea salt

1 teaspoon beef gelatin

1. In a blender, blend the bananas, ice cubes, coconut milk, cacao powder, salt, and gelatin until smooth, roughly 45 seconds.

2. Pour into two 8-ounce glasses and serve immediately.

NOTE: For a creamier smoothie, use frozen bananas and skip the ice cubes.

Strawberry Milk

What kid can resist strawberry-flavored milk? I sure as heck couldn't. I remember gazing with adoration at the rabbit sipping a big old glass of it on the front of the Nesquik container. This quick drink rivals the store-bought version and is much healthier. If your strawberries are very sweet, you can skip the maple syrup.

PREP TIME

5 min

MAKES

2 servings

INGREDIENTS

10 ripe medium strawberries, hulled

2 cups Coconut Milk (page 34)

¼ teaspoon sea salt

¼ teaspoon vanilla extract

1 tablespoon maple syrup (if needed)

1. Place all of the ingredients in a blender. Blend for 1 minute if using a high-powered blender, or 3 to 4 minutes if using a regular blender, until the strawberries have completely disintegrated.

2. Pour into two 8-ounce glasses and serve immediately.

Horchata

When I discovered this cinnamon-spiced Mexican drink as a kid in Arizona, I drank it by the pint. It's traditionally made with rice, and food coloring is often added to make it bright pink or green. I have a weakness for colorful drinks, and this version fits the bill, but it is so much healthier than what I grew up drinking.

INGREDIENTS

½ cup unsweetened shredded coconut

½ teaspoon ground cinnamon

⅛ teaspoon salt

½ teaspoon maple syrup

2 tablespoons beet juice (optional)

2 cups boiling water

1. In a blender, combine the coconut, cinnamon, salt, maple syrup, and beet juice, if using. Add the boiling water and blend for 1 minute if using a high-powered blender, or 3 to 4 minutes if using a regular blender.

2. Strain with a nut milk bag or through cheesecloth into a jar.

3. Let cool for 8 minutes, and then pour into two 8-ounce glasses and serve.

NOTE: If you store leftover horchata in the refrigerator, you may notice that some coconut cream gels at the top. Remove it before drinking (and use it in another dish).

Ginger-Mint Spritzer

The combination of spicy ginger and cool peppermint will make this your favorite summer drink. The ginger-mint syrup is very sweet, so a little goes a long way. And by the way, I'm a teetotaler, but this recipe calls for a splash of tequila like nobody's business.

PREP TIME

10 min

COOK TIME
30 min

MAKES
1 serving

INGREDIENTS

3 cups water

1 (3-inch) piece ginger, peeled and cut into slices ¼ inch thick

¼ cup honey

½ teaspoon organic peppermint flavor

8 ounces sparkling mineral water

ice

fresh mint leaves, for garnish

1. Bring the water to a boil in a large saucepan. Lower the heat to medium, add the ginger and honey, and whisk until well combined. Cook until reduced by half, about 30 minutes.

2. Remove from the heat and whisk in the peppermint flavor. Strain the syrup through cheesecloth into a pint glass jar.

3. Pour 1 tablespoon of the ginger-mint syrup and the mineral water into an 8-ounce glass filled with ice. Garnish with fresh mint leaves and serve immediately.

4. Store the remainder of the syrup in an airtight container in the fridge. It will keep for up to 3 weeks.

Cherry-Lime Spritzer

The combination of cherries and lime juice makes for a great spritzer to cool off on a hot summer day. I love to make this with Rainier cherries, which I consider to be the Brad Pitt of cherries because they're just so dang pretty. My son guzzles this spritzer by the pint.

PREP TIME

10 min

MAKES
4
servings

INGREDIENTS

12 fresh cherries, stemmed and pitted

2 tablespoons lime juice

3 cups sparkling mineral water

1 tablespoon maple syrup

ice

1. In a blender, combine the cherries, lime juice, mineral water, and maple syrup. Blend for 1 minute if using a high-powered blender, or 3 to 4 minutes if using a regular blender.

2. Fill four 8-ounce glasses with ice and pour the spritzer into the glasses. Serve immediately.

Acknowledgments

To Mr. Bejelly — Words cannot express how thankful I am that I get to hold your hand throughout life. Thank you for putting your faith in my mercurial ways and always seeing the truth in this journey together. Thank you for carrying more weight on your shoulders while I was creating this book and for believing in me.

To the Little — It is a joy being your mother. Thank you for being my number-one taste-tester and understanding that I have to take a photo before you can dig in. I want nothing more than for our lives to be filled with sweet memories in the kitchen.

To Mother and Father — Thank you for nurturing my creative side and always believing in me. Mom, the lessons I learned in the kitchen are priceless, and I will always be grateful for how much of a taskmaster you are. I still hear "chop it fine, Kel" every time I dice an onion.

To Glenda — Thank you for crossing my i's and dotting my t's.

To Erich and Michele at Victory Belt and Katherine, my agent — Thank you for seeing the potential in me and believing in my success.

To my wonderful testers — Maxima Miller, Eva Breedijk, Dawn Mercer, Cindy Bean, Tanna Ray, Kathryn Metcalf, Jennifer Klon, Beverly Horner, Joanne Sarkar, Donna Halbrooks, Melissa Mortensen, Connie Taylor, Hannah Pinkerton, Rachel Ochoa, Marie Ysais, Sharon Baharoff, Joanne Sarkar, Tanya Roehlk, Tanya Lenzner, Lisa Gilbert, Krystal Rothbauer, Kristie Bailey, Carrie Hines, Cristy Chuparkoff, Tawna Maiden, Amy Brown, Nick Triantafillou, Kathy Conway, Minh Nguyen, Corrine Johnston.

Your feedback helped me perfect the recipes in this book, and I am forever grateful for that! Maxima, you saved my bacon by testing so many recipes, and I am so grateful to you, my darling sister.

To the amazing men and women in my Paleo bloggers support group — It is an honor and a privilege to be part of such an amazing community of foodie and wellness geniuses. To your every success!

Kelly's Paleo Baking Tutorial

At one time or another, we've all had a family recipe that we wanted to make Paleo-friendly but had no idea how to do so.

I've been there, staring at a pantry full of strange items and wondering how in the world I was going to make cookies or bread for my family. Thankfully, this task is a lot easier than it seems. Instead of just giving you recipes that you can make and enjoy, I want to teach you how to modify your own favorite recipes. There are going to be times on this diet when you wish you could make your Aunt Emily's famous strawberry shortcake, and after you read through this section, it should be a much easier task for you to tackle.

Before we jump into the *Paleo Eats* Paleo-fy School, let's discuss the journey of learning something new. You are already an expert at the art of learning something new. First, you know that you are going to make mistakes. Second, you know that with time and practice, you'll get these techniques down, and eventually re-creating your favorite recipes will be a breeze.

To start, try searching the Internet for a Paleo recipe close to the one you're trying to re-create. My website, *A Girl Worth Saving* (www.agirlworthsaving.net), has a vast library of comfort food recipes that might help you get to the finish line. There are also a plethora of amazing bloggers out there testing and creating recipes that you can tweak slightly or use as a guide to turn your grandma's scone recipe into one you can enjoy on the Paleo diet.

A Primer on Paleo Baking

If I could boil my Paleo baking advice down to one tip, it is this: When re-creating recipes like breads, cakes, pancakes, and waffles, the appearance of the batter should be very similar to the wheat-based version. The difference is that Paleo batters are a touch thicker, so don't thin them!

Now let's get going on the primer. In the next several pages, you'll learn all sorts of tips to help you with your Paleo baking experiments, including how to work with the three most popular Paleo flours: coconut flour, almond flour, and tapioca flour. (You'll find additional information on these flours on pages 16 and 17, too.)

COCONUT FLOUR

Coconut flour has a very heavy, dense texture and is absolutely *nothing like* wheat flour. You have to use a lot of eggs and oil to get it come out light and fluffy. The eggs give it a little rise, and the oil keeps the flour from drying out. You can reduce the number of eggs by substituting ¼ cup of applesauce, puréed sweet potatoes, or fruit for one large egg. The texture lends itself to muffins, cakes, and quick bread. The trick to creating cookies that don't taste like lumpy bread is to keep the amount of coconut flour to less than ¼ cup. I prefer to blend it with almond flour to help give the recipe more weight and binding.

Coconut flour does have a sweet taste that some people don't like, which is another reason I like to use it in combination with almond flour and/or tapioca flour. Honestly, though, after five years on the Paleo diet, I rarely taste it.

Coconut flour is also an incredible thickener, and if you are creating a baked goods recipe and find that it's a bit runnier than it should be, you can add 1 tablespoon of coconut flour, stir, and wait a minute to let the flour thicken. If it's still too runny, add another tablespoon, wait a minute, and repeat until you get the right consistency.

Coconut flour–based baked goods have a shorter shelf life than almond flour–based goods, so freeze leftovers after two days and defrost as needed.

There is no simple formula for substituting coconut flour for wheat flour. I wish I could just say to add a certain amount and it will work, but that would be a lie. As a starter for most coconut flour–only baked goods recipes, I use this formula:

¼ cup coconut flour
+ 2 eggs
+ 1 cup oil
+ 1 cup fruit puree

Then I add any sweeteners, spices, and so on to make it into the intended creation.

Honestly, I hate using a lot of eggs because I don't like eggy-tasting sweets, so I satisfy coconut flour's moisture-loving beast with oil and fruit puree.

When blending coconut flour with other flours, I use anywhere from 2 tablespoons to ¼ cup, depending on the recipe. The more coconut flour you use, the more liquid you are going to have to add to balance it out.

ALMOND FLOUR (BLANCHED, SUPERFINE)

If you don't have a nut allergy, almond flour is the perfect flour to use to Paleo-fy your family recipes. Once you get the technique down, most people will not be able to tell that you have substituted almond flour for white flour in your recipes.

More often than not, you can substitute almond flour for white flour on a 1:1 ratio. But—yeah, there's a *but*—not always. Just as with coconut flour, I cannot give you an easy formula that works 100 percent of the time. If you find that your recipe is too thin after you've mixed everything together, add ¼ cup of almond flour at a time until you get the right consistency.

Almond flour has a higher fat content and is less dense than white flour. When re-creating a recipe that originally used white flour, reduce the fat called for by half and increase the flour by half.

Almond flour is available in different textures. I recommend using blanched, superfine almond flour. Your recipe batter will be smoother, and it won't result in gritty baked goods.

Almond flour is a tricky flour to use when trying to create egg-free recipes because the baked goods tend to be gooier. The best approach varies according to the recipe, of course, but in general I suggest mixing it with coconut flour if you're not using eggs.

Almond meal is a whole other ball game, and I don't recommend using it in baked goods. It has a very gritty texture, so I use it in coatings or to re-create a rough texture in foods.

TAPIOCA FLOUR

Tapioca flour has revolutionized baked goods in the Paleo diet: no other Paleo flour makes bread that's really chewy. It does have a slightly different texture from the store-bought bread that you enjoyed in the past, but trust me, tapioca flour is a close substitute for white flour, and thankfully, it doesn't come with the harmful effects of gluten. If you eat dairy, pão de queijo, a Brazilian cheese bread, is made with tapioca flour and is the closest you will come to the soft rolls you remember from childhood. It inspired my recipe for Garlic Bread Rolls (page 90), which is 100 percent dairy-free. Tapioca flour is excellent for egg-free baking, and you can easily use banana or applesauce as the binder instead of eggs.

However, tapioca flour is tricky to work with. Keep these tips in mind:

1. I only use Bob's Red Mill brand. Sometimes the brand affects how the recipe turns out. I have even had a website reader share that my recipe turned out perfectly, but she ran into issues when she bought a new bag of the same brand of flour. Yes, it keeps you on your toes in the kitchen.

2. If the dough is too soft and/or watery, add more tapioca flour ¼ cup at a time.

3. If the dough will not come together, put it in your food processor or stand mixer and process until a dough forms.

4. If the dough is too stiff, add more oil a tablespoon at a time until the texture has softened.

5. When using tapioca flour as a thickener, whisk it in with the cold ingredients, as it tends to clump in hot liquids.

6. When making sauces with tapioca flour, start off by whisking a teaspoon into warm (not hot) water, and then wait four minutes to see if the consistency is right. If not, add another teaspoon and repeat. Be cautious, though: if you add too much, the texture will be very sticky, and you won't be able to save the recipe.

I am not telling you this to scare you, but to arm you with information and the mindset of an adventurer ready to conquer a new flour. You can also check out my YouTube channel for videos showing how tapioca flour comes together in a recipe and how the finished dough should look.

Can I Substitute . . .

. . . one Paleo flour for another? Many people have asked me if you can substitute coconut flour for almond flour or for tapioca flour. This is a tricky question because yes, you can, but you will have to use completely different amounts of each flour, and the texture of the final dish will be different. Baked goods made with coconut flour are dense, those made with almond flour are moist and light, and those made with tapioca flour are chewy.

I don't recommend substituting one Paleo flour for another until you have a good amount of grain-free baking under your belt. But just as an example, here's a very rough guideline:

¼ cup coconut flour + 1 egg = roughly 1 cup almond flour

1 cup of tapioca flour = roughly ½ cup almond flour

Again, you are getting into recipe creation when you start replacing these flours, and you should expect to make a lot of changes to get to the finish line. But although grain-free baking might seem a touch overwhelming to start, most of the time you can completely fix a recipe that has too much coconut flour or almond flour by simply adding more eggs. The flours are more forgiving than you might believe. With time and practice, you will become a pro.

. . . home-ground nut flour for store-bought? From time to time, I grind whole almonds into a flour and use it in recipes. The thing is, one cup of whole nuts, when ground, does not equal one cup of nut flour. There is also a lot of variation because each time you measure out one cup of nuts, you get a different number of whole nuts. Also, soaked and dehydrated nuts give a different amount of flour than regular nuts.

As a general rule, I double the amount of nut flour needed and grind up that amount of nuts. For instance, if I need one cup of almond flour, I'll grind two cups of almonds, which will yield a bit more than one cup of flour. I use the cup called for in the the recipe and then add more, ¼ cup at a time, until the consistency is correct.

Troubleshooting

Why didn't it work? Cooking is lot like alchemy. You start off with meat, vegetables, spices, and other ingredients, and you end up with a gastronomical experience that's more than the sum of its parts. Of course, that's assuming it's not burned, crumbly, gooey, and so on. If something goes wrong, the problem may be with one of these factors.

The Oven. When we moved into our new home, I was stoked to see we had an expensive, brand-name stove, but later I discovered it was fifteen years old and as temperamental as a preteen. The oven was constantly telling me it was 350°F when it was actually ten degrees higher. If you're finding that your baked goods are coming out burned, dried out, or uneven, it's time to invest in an oven thermometer.

The Humble Measuring Cup. Cooking by weight is much more accurate than cooking by measurement. Depending on how firmly you pack a cup and the amount of moisture in the air, your measurement of 1 cup could be 100 grams one day and 110 grams the next.

Altitude Makes a Difference. Living in Portland, Oregon, I'm fifty feet above sea level. If you live at a higher altitude, the cooking times for the recipes in this book need to be different because of the lower atmospheric pressure. Strangely enough, boiling water at high altitude is actually cooler than boiling water at sea level. If you live at a higher elevation, above 3,500 feet:

- Cooking eggs will take longer because of their high water content. But cook your eggs longer, not at a higher temperature, so they don't burn.

- For recipes that involve braising, stewing, and poaching, you will need to reduce the cook time because water evaporates quicker.

- With baked goods, you will need to reduce the amounts of baking soda, yeast, and baking powder. You will also need to add more eggs or liquid to compensate for the faster evaporation.

The Singular Egg. Eggs are important in baking because they provide binding, leavening, and texture. They're particularly important in recipes that use moisture-loving coconut flour.

One thing I learned pretty quickly when we started raising chickens is that the size of eggs is not uniform. We have a chicken that lays monster 4-inch-long, double-yolk eggs that leave me wondering how she walks after she lays them. I've called for large eggs in all of my recipes, but how you get your eggs—if you raise hens, get them from the farmers market, or buy them at the grocery store—affects their size, and variations in size will affect your batter. The official weight of a large egg is 2 ounces, so if you have eggs that vary in size, you can weigh them and use however many are necessary to get the total weight the recipe calls for.

Having said all this, if you find the batter is dry and crumbly, add another egg. It just might be the only thing you need to tweak.

How to Fix It?

I've found that the batters for grain-free recipes are very similar to their wheat counterparts, just a tad thicker. If you're looking at a cake batter and it is crumbly or very loose and liquidy, something went wrong.

First, did you add the correct amount of each ingredient? I've been guilty of adding a tablespoon when it should have been a teaspoon, or even worse, adding a cup when it should have been ½ cup. If you've added too much of an ingredient, you can either abort (which can be hard to do when you take into account the cost of the ingredients) or work with what you have to get the best result.

If it's too crumbly, I recommend adding more eggs.

If it's lumpy, first try smoothing out the batter with a blender, food processor, or hand mixer, and then add oil a tablespoon at a time until the batter is smooth. If you find that you're adding more than ½ cup of oil, try adding another egg instead.

If it's too liquidy, I recommend adding more of the recipe's main flour, ¼ cup at a time, or adding coconut flour, a tablespoon at a time. Coconut flour does require a minute to set up, so after mixing it in, wait a good minute, then check the consistency and add more if needed.

Remember, Paleo batters are always a touch thicker than batters made with wheat flour, so don't thin them!

Cooking Equivalents and Conversions

If you prefer to use fresh spices or need to scale down a recipe to feed fewer folks, this section provides the conversions that will make it easier to change it up as needed.

FROM DRIED TO FRESH

I prefer to use dried herbs because they last longer and it's much easier to get a precise measurement. However, I know that some people prefer fresh herbs, so here's a helpful chart on dried herbs and their fresh equivalents.

¼ garlic powder = 2 cloves fresh garlic

1 ginger powder = 1 chopped fresh ginger

1½ dried cilantro = 1 chopped fresh cilantro

1 dried rosemary = 1 chopped fresh rosemary

1 dried thyme = 1 chopped fresh thyme

1 dried oregano = 1 chopped fresh oregano

MAKING HALF A RECIPE

¼ → 2

⅓ → 2 +2

½ → ¼

⅔ → ⅓

¾ → 6

1 → ½

½ → ¼

COMMON CONVERSIONS

½ = 30 drops

1 = ⅓ or 60 drops

3 = 1 or ½ fluid ounce

½ = 1½

1 = 3 or ½ fluid ounce

2 = ⅛ or 1 fluid ounce

3 = 1½ fluid ounces or 1 jigger

4 = ¼ or 2 fluid ounces

5⅓ = ⅓ or 5 +1

8 = ½ or 4 fluid ounces

10⅔ = ⅔ or 10 +2

12 = ¾ or 6 fluid ounces

16 = 1 or 8 fluid ounces or ½ pint

⅛ = 2 or 1 fluid ounce

¼ = 4 or 2 fluid ounce

⅓ = 5 +1

⅜ = ¼ +2

½ = 8 or 4 fluid ounces or 1 gill

⅔ = 10 +2

⅝ = ½ +2

¾ = 12 or 6 fluid ounces

⅞ = ¾ +2

1 = 16 or ½ pint or 8 fluid ounces

2 = 1 pint or 16 fluid ounces

1 pint = 2 or 16 fluid ounces

1 quart = 2 pints or 4 or 32 fluid ounces

1 gallon = 4 quarts or 8 pints or 16 or 128 fluid ounces

Substitutions

Trying to figure out what to substitute for non-Paleo ingredients? Here's a short guide.

	SUBSTITUTE
Whole milk	· Homemade Coconut Milk (page 34). It has a very light coconut taste but enough creaminess to use as you would traditionally use milk—in cereal, beverages, etc. · Nut milk, any. It has a very light taste, but those with nut allergies must avoid it.
Heavy whipping cream	Canned, full-fat coconut milk. It has a very strong coconut taste and is very thick and rich.
Sour cream	Cashew Sour Cream (page 62)
Yogurt	Cashew Sour Cream (page 62)
Whipped cream	Whipped Coconut Cream (page 234)
Cream cheese	This one is tough; it depends on the recipe you are trying to re-create. For both hot and cold dishes, I would try coconut cream first. For cold dishes, like no-bake pies, you can also try a nut butter or banana and coconut oil to get the correct texture.
Breadcrumbs	Crushed pork rinds
Fillers in meatloaf, meatballs, and sausage	Crushed pork rinds, coconut flour, or almond flour
Cornstarch	Tapioca flour
All-purpose flour, 1 cup	· ¼ cup to ⅓ cup coconut flour plus 1 large egg. You may also have to add more of the liquid ingredients. · 1 cup blanched, superfine almond flour
Corn syrup, light and dark	Honey
Granulated sugar, 1 cup	· ¼ cup honey* · ¼ cup maple syrup*
Brown sugar	Coconut sugar
Powdered sugar (aka confectioners' sugar)	Homemade powdered sugar (page 60), made with coconut sugar and tapioca flour
Butter or margarine	Palm shortening, leaf lard, or coconut oil
Vegetable oil	Coconut oil, palm shortening, or leaf lard
Peanut butter	Almond butter, cashew butter, or sunflower seed butter**
Soy sauce	Coconut aminos

In conventional baking, honey is substituted for white sugar at a 1:1 ratio and maple syrup is substituted for white sugar at a 1: ¾ ratio, but a lower ratio helps better regulate your blood sugar levels and minimize your insulin response. Start with less honey or maple syrup and increase to taste.

**Sunflower seed butter has a very strong flavor that some people do not like.*

Basic Cooking Terms

Knowing these basic cooking terms will make preparing the recipes in this book easier and help take your cooking to the next level.

Chop: This is one of the simplest and quickest cooking techniques. To chop is to cut food into small pieces. The pieces don't have to be uniform.

Dice: Dicing is similar to chopping, but the pieces are uniform and cubed. The most common size of dice is ¼ inch. A small or fine dice is ⅛ inch, and a large dice is ½ inch. Dice larger than ½ inch are commonly referred to as "cubed," ¾ or 1 inch being the most common size.

To dice an onion, first cut the peeled onion in half lengthwise with a sharp knife. Lay one half facedown on the cutting board and make several horizontal slices with the knife parallel to the cutting board. Then make several slices crosswise to create dice.

To cut long or oval-shaped foods, such as carrots or potatoes, first cut them into ¼- or ½-inch-wide planks, depending on the size of the dice you want. Then stack the planks and cut long strips in the same width. Finally, make crosswise cuts to create dice.

Fold: This technique helps create light, fluffy baked goods. It's a way of blending something light, like whipped egg whites, into something heavy, like a batter. To fold one ingredient into another, use a rubber spatula to scoop down into the center of the bowl and move the spatula up and over, along the base and sides of the bowl, in a circular motion. Turn the bowl and repeat.

Julienne: A pretty word for a very simple cut. To julienne means to cut food into uniform matchsticks, traditionally about 2 inches long and ⅛ inch wide, although they can also be ¼ or even ½ inch wide. I often use the phrase "cut into strips" when I'm talking about this technique. To julienne a food, cut it into slices, then stack the planks and cut long strips of the desired width. Carrots, celery, and bell peppers are often julienned, but it can be done with most vegetables.

Marinate: To marinate a food is to soak it in a mixture of spices, oil, and possibly an acid, such as vinegar or fruit juice, to make it more tender and flavorful. Marinating times vary from a half hour to several days, depending on the dish and the food being marinated.

Mince: To mince is to finely chop a food into tiny pieces. This technique is typically associated with garlic and onions.

Mix, blend: These are probably the most used terms in this book! They basically mean to combine two or more ingredients by hand or with a blender or mixer until completely smooth and uniform.

Sauté: To sauté is to cook a food in a small amount of fat. This is often done over high heat so that you can quickly move to the next step.

Simmer: To simmer is to cook a liquid at a temperature high enough that tiny bubbles begin to break the surface, but not so high that it begins to boil.

Slice: To slice is to cut completely through an object. Think of slicing cheese or bread. The same principle applies to veggies, meat, and fruit.

DICE

CHOP

MINCE

JULIENNE

SLICE

Online Resources

Sites on the Paleo Diet, Nutrition, and Fitness

Mark's Daily Apple (marksdailyapple.com): An incredible resource on the Paleo/primal lifestyle. It's where I learned everything I know about this diet.

Real Food Liz (realfoodliz.com): Liz Wolfe is funny, sassy, and smart as a whip. She breaks down the real truth on nutrition and health.

Robb Wolf (robbwolf.com): Another fantastic site that covers the Paleo diet from A to Z.

AIP Resources

Autoimmune Paleo (autoimmune-paleo.com): Mickey Trescott has some amazing recipes and is a great resource for learning more about AIP.

The Paleo Mom (www.thepaleomom.com): Sarah Ballantyne is a health genius in my book, and her site focuses on recipes and the science behind achieving wellness through the Paleo diet and the Autoimmune Protocol.

Recipe Sites

A Girl Worth Saving (www.agirlworthsaving.net): My website, where I share grain-free recipes, how-to tutorials, and cooking tips.

Paleo on a Budget (paleoonabudget.com): If you're trying to save money on the Paleo diet, you need to visit Liz's site. She has meal plans, coupon round-ups, and delicious recipes to help you stretch your budget.

The Paleo Parents (paleoparents.com): Stacy Toth and Matt McCarry share delicious Paleo recipes, and you get a glimpse into their family's life on the diet.

Rubies and Radishes (www.rubiesandradishes.com): Arsy Vartanian shares a variety of Paleo recipes.

The Spunky Coconut (www.thespunkycoconut.com): A woman with a sweet tooth similar to my own, Kelly Brozyna shares amazing desserts for the Paleo lifestyle.

Zenbelly (www.zenbelly.com): Simone Miller is a chef who creates tantalizing Paleo recipes.

Shopping

A Girl Worth Saving (www.agirlworthsaving.net): I buy a lot of my pantry items from Amazon and make use of their Subscribe & Save program to help keep costs down. You can find my favorites in my shop.

Eat Wild (www.eatwild.com): Find farms in your area for purchasing grass-fed meats and other products.

Local Harvest (www.localharvest.org): Locate CSAs, farmers markets, and small farms in your area.

PANTRY

Artisana (www.artisanafoods.com): Coconut butter

Bob's Red Mill (www.bobsredmill.com): Tapioca flour, baking soda

Bragg (bragg.com): Apple cider vinegar

Coconut Secret (www.coconutsecret.com): Coconut aminos and coconut sugar

Eden Foods (www.edenfoods.com): Apple butter

Equal Exchange (www.equalexchange.coop): 70% cacao bittersweet chocolate chips

Fatworks Foods (www.fatworksfoods.com): Lard, duck fat, and tallow

Great Lakes (www.greatlakesgelatin.com): Grass-fed beef gelatin

Hidden Springs Maple (www.hiddenspringsmaple.com): Grade B maple syrup

Inka Chips (www.inkacrops.com): Plantain chips

JK Gourmet (www.jkgourmet.com): Blanched, superfine almond flour

Natural Value (www.naturalvalue.com): Coconut milk

Navitas Naturals (navitasnaturals.com): Cacao powder, coconut palm sugar

Red Boat Fish Sauce (redboatfishsauce.com): Fish sauce

Red Star (www.redstaryeast.com): Yeast

The Spice Lab (shop.thespicelab.com): Himalayan salt

Sunspire (www.sunspire.com): 100% cacao unsweetened baking chocolate

Tropical Traditions (www.tropicaltraditions.com): Coconut flour, palm shortening, expeller-pressed coconut oil, raw honey

U.S. Wellness Meats (www.grasslandbeef.com): Pastured meats, pork rinds, organ meat sausages

Wellbee's (www.wellbees.com): Blanched, superfine almond flour

The Wizard's Organic Saucery (www.edwardandsons.com/thewizards_info.itml): Worcestershire sauce

TOOLS

Anchor Hocking (www.anchorhocking.com): Loaf pans

Blendtec (www.blendtec.com): High-speed professional blenders

Chicago Metallic (www.chicagometallicbakeware.com): Bakeware

Cuisinart (www.cuisinart.com): Food processors, ice cream makers, electric hand mixers

Hamilton Beach (www.hamiltonbeach.com): Slow cookers

Le Creuset (www.lecreuset.com): Enameled cast-iron pans

Lodge (www.lodgemfg.com): Cast-iron pans

Paderno (paderno.com): Spiral slicers

Silpat (silpat.com): Nonstick silicone baking mats

Wilton (www.wilton.com): 6-inch cake pans

THE BASICS

26 Barbecue Sauce

28 Ketchup

30 Homemade Mayo

32 Sweet-and-Sour Sauce

34 Coconut Milk

36 Teriyaki Sauce

38 Ranch Dressing

40 Honey Mustard

42 Tahini Sauce

44 Chicken Bone Broth

46 Hot Sauce

48 Pesto

50 Slow Cooker Spaghetti Sauce

52 Thai Almond Sauce

54 Mushroom Gravy

56 Salsa Verde

58 Strawberry Jam

60 Powdered Sugar

62 Cashew Sour Cream

BREADS, WRAPS, & PASTRIES

66
Caramel Apple
Cinnamon Rolls

68
Cherry Toaster
Pastries

70
Apple Fritters

72
Pizza Crust

74
Sweet Bread

76
Yeasted Biscuits

78
Grain-Free Wraps

80
Sweet Potato Biscuits

82
Basic Pie Crust

84
Hamburger Buns

86
Skillet Cornbread

88
Breadsticks

90
Garlic Bread Rolls

92
Raisin Bread

BREAKFAST

96 Coconut Cinnamon Cereal

98 Crustless Quiche

100 Banana Pancakes

102 French Toast

104 Mock Oatmeal

106 Breakfast Burrito

108 Breakfast Sausage

110 Granola

112 Over-Easy Eggs Benedict

114 Berry Parfait

116 Broccolini and Sweet Potato Omelet

MAINS

120
Oven-Baked
Dry-Rubbed Ribs

122
Meatloaf

124
Chicken Katsu

126
Pancit

128
Sloppy Joes

130
Chicken Parmesan

132
Salmon Cakes

134
Ginger Chicken

136
Pepper Steak

138
Southern Fried
Chicken

140
Lamb Gyro Burgers

142
Chili

144
Pho Ga

146
Kung Pao Chicken

148
Chicken Enchilada
Casserole

150
Chicken Pot Pie

152
Sweet-and-Sour
Meatballs

154
Easy Yellow Curry

156
Salisbury Steak

158
Oven-Baked
Chicken Balls

160
Roasted Chicken

162
Roasted Turkey

164
Clam Chowder

166
Chicken and
Dumplings

168
Pierogi

170
Creamy Chicken and
Broccolini Bake

SIDES & SALADS

174 Cranberry Sauce

176 Creamy Cucumber Dill Salad

178 Mashed "Potatoes"

180 Garlic Fried Rice

182 Hush Puppies

184 Bucha Onion Rings

186 Honey Ginger Carrots

188 Creamed Brussels Sprouts

190 Rosemary Garlic Summer Squash

192 Duchess Sweet Potatoes

194 Spinach Nuggets

196 Sweet Potato Salad

198 Creamy Caesar Salad

200 Braised Red Cabbage and Apples

202 Thanksgiving Dressing

204 Green Bean Casserole

206 Hummus

208 Creamy Grits

210 Zucchini Noodles

212 Sweet Potato Fries

DESSERTS

216

Chocolate Chip
Cookies

218

Carrot Cake

220

Vanilla Frosting

222

"Oatmeal" Raisin
Cookies

224

No-Bake Chocolate
Raspberry
"Cheesecake"

226

Peach Cobbler

228

Grasshopper
Pudding

230

Almond Butter
Sandwich Cookies

232

Banana Cream Pie

234

Whipped Coconut
Cream

236

Key Lime Pie

238

Devil's Food Cake

240

Chocolate-Covered
Strawberries

242

Apple Pie Ice Cream

244

Apple Pie

246

Cream-Filled
Chocolate Cupcakes

248

Chocolate Sandwich
Cookies

250

Creamy Hazelnut
and Chocolate Pie

252

Unfried Ice Cream

254

Pecan Pie

256

Pumpkin Pie

258

Kitchen Sink Cookies

DRINKS

262

Salted Chocolate
Smoothie

264

Strawberry Milk

266

Horchata

268

Ginger-Mint Spritzer

270

Cherry-Lime Spritzer

SPECIAL OCCASIONS

 Holiday

Mushroom Gravy

Roasted Turkey

Cranberry Sauce

Mashed "Potatoes"

Thanksgiving Dressing

Green Bean Casserole

Pecan Pie

Pumpkin Pie

Valentine's Day

No-Bake Chocolate Raspberry "Cheesecake"

Chocolate-Covered Strawberries

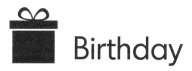

Birthday

218
Carrot Cake

224
No-Bake Chocolate Raspberry "Cheesecake"

238
Devil's Food Cake

246
Cream-Filled Chocolate Cupcakes

Game day

120
Oven-Baked Dry-Rubbed Ribs

184
Bucha Onion Rings

196
Sweet Potato Salad

212
Sweet Potato Fries

AIP RECIPES

34
Coconut Milk

36
Teriyaki Sauce

54
Mushroom Gravy

58
Strawberry Jam

68
Cherry Toaster Pastries

126
Pancit

134
Ginger Chicken

174
Cranberry Sauce

186
Honey Ginger Carrots

188
Creamed Brussels Sprouts

190
Rosemary Garlic Summer Squash

210
Zucchini Noodles

212
Sweet Potato Fries

Index